General editor: Graham Handley MA Ph D

Brodie's Notes on Jane Austen's

Northanger Abbey

Graham Handley MA Ph D
Formerly Principal Lecturer in English, College of All Saints, Tottenham

Pan Books London and Sydney

This revised edition published 1986 by Pan Books Ltd
Cavaye Place, London SW10 9PG
9 8 7 6 5 4 3 2 1

ISBN 0 330 50227 1
Photoset by Parker Typesetting Service, Leicester
Printed and bound in Great Britain by
Richard Clay (The Chaucer Press) Ltd, Bungay, Suffolk

Contents

Page references are to the Pan Classics edition of *Northanger Abbey* but as references are also given to particular chapters, the Notes may be used with any edition of the book.

Preface

The intention throughout this study aid is to stimulate and guide, to encourage the reader's *involvement* in the text, to develop disciplined critical responses and a sure understanding of the main details in the chosen text.

Brodie's Notes provide a summary of the plot of the play or novel followed by act, scene or chapter summaries each of which will have an accompanying critical commentary designed to underline the most important literary and factual details. Textual notes will be explanatory or critical (sometimes both), defining what is difficult or obscure on the one hand, or stressing points of character, style or plot on the other. Revision questions will be set on each act or group of chapters to test the student's careful application to the text of the prescribed book.

The Notes also provide a critical examination of the author's art. This will cover such major elements as characterization, style, structure, setting, theme(s) or any other aspect of the book which the editor considers needs close study. The paramount aim is to send the student back to the text. Each study aid will include a series of general questions which require a detailed knowledge of the set book; the first of these questions will have notes by the editor of what *might* be included in written answer. A short list of books considered useful as background reading for the student will be provided at the end.

Graham Handley

Literary terms used in these notes

There is little need to employ a literary vocabulary when examining the novels of Jane Austen. Certain terms, however, do help to define her style and her method in *Northanger Abbey*.

Irony This is a favourite Jane Austen usage. At one level it is the humorous or sarcastic use of words to imply the opposite of what they usually mean. Thus Isabella is presented ironically because so much of what she says – in terms of friendship, loyalty, behaviour – is the *opposite* of what she does or intends. The term further embraces incongruity or irrationality (almost all the utterances of John Thorpe are forms of irony) and incongruity between what is expected to be and what actually is (as in Catherine's Gothic expectations of the Abbey – the chest – the writing – and what is finally normality).

Satire Writing (generally) in which topical issues, folly, or evil are held up to scorn or ridiculed by means of irony. In *Northanger Abbey* the Gothic novel, pretentiousness (the General, or Mrs Allen's constant obsession with dress) are satirized. Henry Tilney ridicules the Gothic novel, as does the author herself.

The author and her work

Jane Austen was born in December 1775 at Steventon in Hampshire where her father George Austen was rector; here she spent her childhood and young womanhood. Her father, who was later to recognize his daughter's unquestionable talents, took pupils and prepared them for Oxford, where two of his sons also studied. Her mother was a keen gardener, had a strong sense of humour, and suffered from lengthy bouts of ill-health. The Austens were a close family. The eldest son James had a curacy, and later succeeded his father at Steventon; while still a boy the next brother Edward was adopted and brought up by well-to-do cousins at Godmersham in Kent; Henry, next in age, was certainly close to Jane in terms of sympathy, sharing her delightful sense of humour and the quality of her wit. Closest of all was her sister Cassandra, to whom many of Jane's letters are written and with whom she shared strong bonds of sympathy and affection; Cassandra was not above mocking her sister in a tone that would certainly have been appreciated: 'You are indeed the finest comic writer of the present age.' Jane's two other brothers Charles and Frank entered the Navy, where both achieved very high rank.

Jane was encouraged to write, her father even corresponding with a publisher on her account, and she often read aloud – particularly her early burlesques – to Cassandra. They were an engaging, attractive and largely unquarrelsome family and, after their father's death, all the sons helped to provide for their mother. In 1782 Jane and Cassandra were sent to stay at a school in Reading, though two years later they were certainly back at home; by this time James was at Oxford. Their father's sister, who married a Frenchman, later became strongly attached to the Austens at Steventon. Her husband was executed in 1794, and it was probably through her that Jane learned much of the world outside Steventon.

Elsewhere in these notes we refer to the literary influences that helped to form Jane Austen's style, but in these impressionable years she was certainly reading Johnson, Goldsmith, Crabbe and Cowper and a host of travel books. Most important of all (and particularly for students of *Northanger Abbey*), she read all the novels she could lay her hands on, and these were many and various. She began to write burlesques or parodies of many of her contemporary writers, almost anticipating Thackeray's own published experiments in this vein some sixty years later. Obviously she wrote much before she was sixteen years old and her juvenilia have been published with editorial commentaries in *Volume the First*, the *Second* and *Third*. The first one was probably left to her brother Charles, but the second volume is *Love and Friendship*, in part told in letters, the form Jane inherited from that great novelist of the eighteenth century, Samuel Richardson, and also from other writers enamoured of the epistolary style. Jane visited her brother Edward in 1794, and again at Godmersham in 1798; in 1797 Cassandra's fiancé died. There is some evidence that *Elinor and Marianne* was written before 1796 in the epistolary mode; it was later re-drafted as *Sense and Sensibility*. *Lady Susan* too was composed in the form of letters, while *First Impressions* was finished in 1797 and offered by Mr Austen to the London publisher Cadell, who turned it down, though the members of the family who heard all or parts of it read were highly appreciative of it. By 1798 Jane was well on with *Susan*, later to suffer considerable revision and to appear as *Northanger Abbey*.

Mr and Mrs Austen were bent on retiring to Bath, and the family certainly visited Ramsgate and Lyme Regis, location of the memorable scene in *Persuasion* when Louisa Musgrove falls off the Cobb and is seriously injured. The Austens settled in Bath just after the turn of the century, and Jane is thought to have had an unhappy love affair shortly after this: the gentleman died. Be that as it may, Jane never really liked Bath, but by 1803 she had revised the early version of *Northanger Abbey*. It was sold to the London publisher Crosby but was not published; nothing more was heard of *Susan*, as it was then called.

The fragment *The Watsons* was begun in 1803, but Jane was to suffer the grievous loss of her friend Mrs Lefroy in 1804, and of her father at the beginning of 1805. During this period she was depressed; in addition to family burdens, it must be remembered that she had received virtually no recognition as an author outside her own family. Her letters throughout this period still reflect her interest in people and how acutely she was sketching them. She has written how thankful she was to leave Bath for Clifton ('with what happy feelings of Escape'). This was in 1806, and in 1807 the family removed to Southampton, where they were to stay for the next three years. They became close again to Edward at Godmersham, and when his wife died leaving eleven children, Jane and Cassandra found themselves constantly employed as aunts to this band of nephews and nieces.

By April 1809 Jane was in touch again with Crosby over *Susan*; Crosby said she could have her manuscript back for what he had paid for it, but that he would prevent anyone else from publishing it. Obviously Jane had kept a copy, which she used for her own revision, since she didn't get Crosby's back until some years later. In 1809 Jane moved with her sister and mother to Chawton in Hampshire, and she still found herself happily in communication with a number of the younger members of the family. Some of these have left sympathetic and affectionate pictures of their aunt, who was generally happy in her life at Chawton.

By early 1811 *Sense and Sensibility* was to be published, and she was already revising *Pride and Prejudice*. In 1813 *Pride and Prejudice* was also to appear, and with the arrival of her own copy Jane could write to Cassandra, 'I have got my own darling child from London.' How much she loved the character Elizabeth Bennet she has told us, for her letters from this period onwards are in some measure concerned with her own writing and with criticism. She wrote, as we know, in the sitting-room, and it is apparent that *Sense and Sensibility, Pride and Prejudice* and *Mansfield Park* were being dealt with at revision or proof level all at the same time. What she wrote was published anonymously and, according to her brother Henry, she held back with each book, 'till time and many perusals had satisfied her that the charm of recent composition was dissolved'.

Mansfield Park appeared in 1814, followed in 1815 by *Emma*, which received not only Scott's generous review, but also the accolade from the Prince Regent's librarian J. S. Clarke, granting Jane Austen permission to dedicate any future work to the Prince. He even went on to suggest to her that she might like to write 'an historical romance, illustrative of the history of the august House of Coburg'. Her horizons, though narrower in terms of geographical compass, were perhaps wider in terms of the human heart. Henry got back the copyright of *Northanger Abbey*, and in 1816 Jane drafted the Advertisement for the novel, which was to be printed posthumously with the text. But she had another novel on her hands, for *Persuasion* had been begun; she finished it in July of 1816, though she cancelled one chapter which was virtually completely redrafted. This novel and *Northanger Abbey* were put aside, and work on *Sanditon* begun in January 1817, though by March Jane was very ill; in May she went with Cassandra to Winchester, where she could receive good medical attention. It was of no avail, and on 18 July she died, leaving *Northanger Abbey* and *Persuasion* to be published in the following year.

Thus lived and died in unremarkable and retired obscurity one of the greatest novelists in the English language. Throughout her writings her moral stance is clear, uncompromising in its perspective, never sententious or smug; she brought to the English novel a new status, thus preparing the way for the great writers of the nineteenth century, like Dickens, George Eliot and Hardy. It has been said that her canvas was narrow, and there is no doubt that she would have acknowledged this; such great events of her time as the French revolution and the ensuing wars, excesses, idealisms and struggles, find no place in her work. But her range encompassed the essential novelist's material, the affairs of the human heart; and with refinement of style and a meticulous observation of character in action and interaction, she brought to fictional characters a closer and deeper scrutiny than they had hitherto received in books.

Jane Austen learned much from those who had written before her, but she imposed her own compactness of form, and gave to her characters a consistent psychology and development that was to influence not only the 19th-century novelists but those who were to write from the consciousness of character in the twentieth. Those who feel that her writings are the skilful but narrow work of an old maid should ask themselves if sexual passion has ever been depicted so strongly – not indulgently, not salaciously, not sensationally – as in the feelings of Darcy for Elizabeth Bennet. The conventions within which Jane lived demanded a certain code of conduct and the inexplicit acknowledgement of what must not be uttered or seen. Yet her awareness encompasses it all, and we know she knows, and that she intends us to know, that the gloss of polite conversation cannot hide people's basic motives. Her way is to be ironic without being cruel, satirical without being complacent, wise without being pretentious and, above all, humane and understanding in her attitude towards the human condition. The purity of her dialogue stands the test of our own time; to translate her to film, stage or television is not to translate but merely to accept – our script-writers cannot improve her.

Jane's spirit is in many ways a comic one, and we might here invoke Meredith's words in his *Essay on Comedy*. 'The laughter of Comedy is impersonal and of unrivalled politeness.' Her country house and parsonage and Bath society seem unaware of tragedy: Yet Jane Austen's faith leads her to show us life as it is, and she steers between the extremes of vinegar and saccharine by the simple expedient of being true to her ear and her eye; they never let her down.

The Gothic novel and other literary influences

The Gothic novel was the predominant literary vogue of the 1790s, with Mrs Radcliffe as its chief English exponent, and a glut of translations from the German also appeared. Mrs Radcliffe, a cultivated and deliberate literary artist, was obviously influenced by Horace Walpole, whose *Castle of Otranto* – almost the prototype Gothic tale – had appeared as early as 1765. From then on the writers in this style of fiction depended on a number of tried and trusted bases on which to rear their tales, what J. M. S. Tompkins has called 'prisons, ghosts, escapes' and the whole paraphernalia of 'imaginative terror'. In her superb study (*The Popular Novel in England 1770–1830*) she draws attention to the crudeness of the German stories, which are sometimes political and anti-clerical in origin and intention, often dealing with secret societies, and also drawing upon alchemy and folk magic. But in relation to *Northanger Abbey* they are of small account, for *The Mysteries of Udolpho* is to *Northanger Abbey* what *Pamela* is to *Joseph Andrews*, the *raison d'être*, the mainspring of inspiration and the pivot of satire. There is of course more to it than that: '*Northanger Abbey* demonstrates the opinion of an informed critic regarding the popular novels of her day.'

Mrs Radcliffe brought delicacy and dignity to the Gothic mode, a literary consciousness that provides a contrast to the violent scenes and atrocities of some of the German equivalents, which were closely related to supernaturalism and folklore, with sprites and witches sometimes appearing. Miss Tompkins has asserted the appeal of Gothic fiction as succinctly, probably, as it can be put:

> It was a folly, run up without any consideration of the need of reasonable beings, a glaring and picturesque façade on the edge of a precipice, uninhabitable by flesh and blood, or even by authentic ghosts. Such as it was, however, it was for the time being immensely stimulating to the cramped fancy of the age. (*The Popular Novel in England* p.247).

Mrs Radcliffe was greatly praised by her contemporaries (among them Coleridge), and her work abounds in descriptions of the picturesque, on the one hand, and in promoting responses of terror and awe on the other. Miss Tompkins has called her work the 'day-dreams of a mind at once fastidious and audacious'. She made romance and the supernatural respectable, with the scenic descriptions interspersed between the pivots of sudden surprise and terror on which the action of her plots turned. Characterization that bears any relationship to reality is not Mrs Radcliffe's strong suit: her heroines are inevitably good, innocent, and often devout; there are benevolent noblemen and conventional attendants. But perhaps we should remember that she was writing at a time immediately following a different kind of horror, namely that of the French Revolution (1789) and the insecurity consequent upon it. Probably for this reason she and her compeers provided a kind of escapism, indicating symbolically the deep-rooted fears of the times. The settings, referred to in *Northanger Abbey*, are those of the South of France, the Alps, Italy; and mystery and supernatural manifestation often attend upon such scenes. Mrs Radcliffe indeed, was able to combine beauty and terror. Here is a representative example from Chapter 5 of *The Mysteries of Udolpho* (1794):

> On the other side of the valley, immediately opposite to the spot where the travellers rested, a rocky pass opened towards Gascony. Here no sign of cultivation appeared. The rocks of granite, that screened the glen, rose abruptly from their base, and stretched their barren points to the clouds, unvaried with woods, and uncheered even by a hunter's cabin. Sometimes, indeed, a gigantic larch threw its long shade over the precipice, and here and there a cliff reared on its brow a monumental cross, to tell the traveller the fate of him who had ventured hither before. This spot seemed the very haunt of banditti; and Emily, as she looked down upon it, almost expected to see them stealing out from some hollow cave to look for their prey. Soon after an object not less terrific struck her – a gibbet standing on a point of rock near the entrance of the pass, and immediately over one of the crosses she had before observed. These were hieroglyphics that told a plain and dreadful story.

This extract is given in full in order that some critical justice may be accorded to Mrs Radcliffe, for the style alone is worthy of comment. It is scenic painting, but with a genuine feeling for words and atmosphere; what is missing is of course a sense of reality. We are in the world of romance, but it is a world both threatened and beautiful. Such scenery is often the background to the Gothic edifice, with its overlay of mystery, terror, secrecy, the supernatural. To these influences the innocent heroine is often exposed, her sensitivity and the forces working upon her imagination predisposing her to taste the possibilities that in Gothic fiction sometimes become terrible fact. One can see from this how close to such a conventional heroine (despite Jane Austen's ironic disclaimers at the beginning) Catherine is when she arrives at Northanger Abbey. The key here, as in Mrs Radcliffe, is a series of evocations of atmosphere – storm, wind, an unusual chest, a manuscript. But in fact Catherine is more enterprising than any of Mrs Radcliffe's heroines were likely to be, since she is capable of positive action and is not just receptive of events. Again we must refer to Miss Tompkins for further definition of Mrs Radcliffe's method:

> The *raison d'être* of her books is not a story, not a character, not a moral Truth but a mood, the mood of a sensitive dreamer before Gothic buildings and picturesque scenery.

Emily's stay at Udolpho is burlesqued by Catherine's stay at Northanger Abbey; Adeline's reading of the manuscript in *The Romance of the Forest* has its parody equivalent in Catherine's guttering candle which merely puts off her perusal of the washing bill. And Catherine is as innocent, and as protected by that innocence, as any Gothic heroine. The technical machinery of *The Mysteries of Udolpho* is not dissimilar from that used by Jane Austen in *Northanger Abbey*: in the latter there are mysteries, which are explained; there is knocking or footsteps (which prove to be Henry, Eleanor or the maid); and there is the author's mockery of sustained suspension – though it must be allowed that Henry Tilney himself was riveted by *The Mysteries of Udolpho* despite his own cynical appraisal of the genre.

In another sense the wide vistas of natural beauty described by Mrs Radcliffe have a corollary in the descriptions which follow the walk to Beechen Cliff or the journey to Woodston; the scale is different, but here the small and natural approximate in their lyrical effect on Catherine to the tranquillity enjoyed in Swiss and Italian backgrounds by the heroines of Mrs Radcliffe. It has been pointed out that the Gothic pile was thought to be a suitable home for a hero, and this, after all, is Henry's role in the novel; Catherine is thus really conditioned by a variety of fictional associations into thinking that there is evil concealed in the Abbey, and the General has all the attributes to fit a highly overwrought interpretation. But if Jane Austen is critical of the Gothic romance and its effects, we can see from the above that she mingles burlesque with some of the main facets of the better romances as straight treatment.

Since Mrs Radcliffe and the Gothic novels mentioned early in

Northanger Abbey provide a genuine comic element in the novel, it would only be right to draw attention to the fact that *Northanger Abbey* is a literary work markedly influenced by the variety, even the catholicity, of Jane Austen's own reading. Even as early as the end of the first chapter there are quotations – and misquotations – three from Shakespeare, one from Gray's *Elegy Written in a Country Churchyard* (perhaps the greatest single poem of the eighteenth century) and one each from Pope and Thomson. The choice indicates the influence upon Jane Austen of the great 18th-century writers and our finest dramatist; scattered throughout the pages of *Northanger Abbey* we come across other indications of her reading and her tastes. She quite obviously admires Richardson – hence the acknowledgement of *Sir Charles Grandison*. She was also known to appreciate Dr Johnson and Cowper, while there is more than one reference to Fanny Burney who, without having Jane's succinctness and wit, was cast in the same elegant stylistic mould as her great successor.

For the purposes of these notes the Pan edition has been used as a text, but Professor Ehrenpreis acknowledges, as must any Jane Austen scholar, the pioneer work of Dr R. W. Chapman in Jane Austen studies. The great Oxford edition of her work under his editorship was issued in 1923, and the volume containing *Northanger Abbey* and *Persuasion* is a mine of background information on those works, which the interested student should not hesitate to explore. Here we are concerned with Part I of the General Index which deals with literary allusions to be found in the novels and the letters. These reveal a wide reading in travel, in poetry and in plays, not merely from the eighteenth century and earlier but from contemporaries as well. Thus we learn that Jane had read much Byron (an exact contemporary) and admired Maria Edgeworth, who was writing when she was; she greatly admired Crabbe, and was reading him at the most fruitful period of her own creative activity, i.e. from 1810–11 onwards. She disapproved apparently of doctrinaire novelists like Godwin but admired the poetry of Scott. It must be remembered that *Waverley* was not written until 1814, so that Jane Austen's appreciation of him was confined to his poetry, some of which she parodied. When she came to read *Waverley* she actually wrote that 'Walter Scott has no business to write novels.'

The object of this brief examination is merely to indicate that Jane Austen was more than well read; she read in depth, having, of course, her own subjective responses but also a good deal of objective rational judgement such as one might expect from one steeped in 18th-century literature. *Northanger Abbey* is much more than a skit on the Gothic novel or on Bath society or an extended exercise in burlesque: it is all of these, but behind it lies a wise and informed mind, with wisdom culled from life and from the literature she loved, as well as the literature she laughed at.

Scott's generous words on *Emma* apply fittingly and tellingly to *Northanger Abbey*, and when he wrote them he had in mind not only Jane Austen's powers of observation but also the literary heritage to which we have referred in some detail in this section:

> Accordingly a style of novel has arisen, within the last fifteen or twenty years, differing from the former in the points upon which the interest hinges; neither alarming our credulity nor amusing our imagination by wild variety of incident, or by those pictures of romantic affection and sensibility, which were formerly as certain attributes of fictitious characters as they are of rare occurrence among those who actually live and die. The substitute for these excitements, which had lost much of their poignancy by the repeated and injudicious use of them, was the art of copying from nature as she really exists in the common walks of life, and presenting to the reader, instead of the splendid scenes of an imaginary world, a correct and striking representation of that which is daily taking place around him. (Sir Walter Scott *Quarterly Review*, 1815–16).

Background and plot

Background

In the 'Advertisement, By The Authoress', Jane Austen refers to the fact that *Northanger Abbey* was 'finished in the year 1803, and intended for immediate publication'. It thus occupies at least in part (if we allow for later revisions) the time of her sojourn in Bath. There is little point here in either adding to that or providing a map of Bath for the period, since the main topographical references are glossed in the textual notes (see pp.23–57). However, the critic R. W. Chapman does quote interesting information from *The Historic and Local New Bath Guide* for 1802, which gives us some indication of that aspect of the social life of the spa perhaps most interesting to Catherine and Isabella:

> There are two Dress Balls every week, viz. on Monday at the New Rooms (referred to in the text as the Upper Rooms), and on Friday at the Lower Rooms . . . There are also two Fancy Balls every week, viz. at the Lower Rooms on Tuesday, and at the New Rooms on Thursday . . . And nine Subscription Concerts, and three Choral Nights, in the Winter at the New Rooms, on Wednesday . . .

Theatre performances were generally on Tuesdays, Thursdays and Saturdays. But if Bath is the centre of activity, Catherine's home in Wiltshire has been given a fictitious name, as has Northanger Abbey in Gloucestershire, and Woodston, the location of Henry's living. There would seem to be little point here in hunting out the original locations, since Jane Austen is concerned more with people *in* places than with the places themselves. *Persuasion* shares with *Northanger Abbey* a satirical view of life in Bath at the height of its fashionable popularity, and in this sense the background is important. We know that two of Jane Austen's homes, Steventon and Chawton, were much loved by her, certainly because they embodied the luxury of retirement, reading, walking and gardening away from the fashionable glare she distrusted – and the two novels referred to above indicate the nature of this distrust. Her letters from Bath are sparse, but the tone is not enthusiastic:

> *Wednesday* Another stupid party last night; perhaps if larger they might be less intolerable; but here there were only just enough to make one card table, with six people to look on and talk nonsense to each other.

One is forced to the conclusion that the satirical nature of *Northanger Abbey* had the Gothic novel for its literary background and the resort of fashionable society for its social and moral ethos.

Plot

The plot of *Northanger Abbey* is relatively straightforward, in common with all of Jane Austen's novels. Catherine Morland – fourth child of the ten born to a clergyman and his wife in Fullerton, Wiltshire – is taken to Bath by her parents' friends, Mr and Mrs Allen, for a stay of six weeks. Shortly after her arrival there, she meets a young man of good family, Henry Tilney a clergyman, while Mrs Allen renews her acquaintance with an old school-friend, a Mrs Thorpe, who is now a widow. Mrs Thorpe's daughter Isabella, a very pretty, but loud and ostentatious girl, immediately attaches herself to Catherine, whom she and the others declare to be very like her brother James. Catherine remembers that James has become friendly with one John Thorpe at Oxford, and soon these two come to Bath. Thorpe turns out to be a bore, interested only in his horse and gig; James proves to be enamoured of Isabella – which is what she has been continually hinting to the unsuspecting Catherine.

Catherine, despite the close attentions of Isabella, wishes to see Henry Tilney again, and looks for him in the various rooms and at the theatre. Later she does meet him again, and his sister Eleanor, but she is bothered by the unwelcome proximity of John Thorpe. She arranges to go for a walk with the Tilneys if the weather is fine, but is persuaded by her brother, Isabella and John to go for what proves to be an abortive drive; just as she is leaving she sees that the Tilneys have called for her and she begs John Thorpe to stop the gig, but he ignores her. Catherine hastens to apologize to Henry when she sees him at the theatre, and though he is initially severe, he softens in response to her obvious sincerity. John Thorpe has been talking to the Tilneys' father General Tilney about Catherine, and, as she learns much later, representing her, and the Allens, as being very rich. Meanwhile James and Isabella wish to become engaged, and the Morland parents give their consent provided that the young couple wait for some three years, when James will have a living of some £400 per annum. This seems very good to Catherine, but Isabella (and her mother) are disappointed that it is not more. Before this Catherine and the Tilneys walk around Beechen Cliff (they were nearly thwarted again by John Thorpe's possessiveness of Catherine), and the Thorpes and James, with one of Isabella's sisters, drive to Clifton.

General Tilney has now made up his mind that Catherine is some kind of heiress (though this is not revealed until the final pages of the novel) and invites her to accompany him, his son and daughter, for a stay at their home, Northanger Abbey. Before this happens, though, Catherine has been somewhat upset by Isabella's behaviour. Captain Frederick Tilney, the elder brother, has made his appearance in Bath and immediately begins to flirt intimately with Isabella. Catherine notices this, but also notices that on her last night in Bath Isabella and James appear to be on the very good terms expected of an engaged couple.

Catherine goes to Northanger and after a couple of days is shown over the Abbey and the gardens and grounds. She feels that there is some mystery surrounding the death of Mrs Tilney some years previously (suspecting the General, whom she does not trust, of making away with her). Henry has gone to his living at Woodston for a couple of days, but returns unexpectedly to find Catherine visiting his late mother's bedroom. He reads her mind and correctly deduces what she has been thinking. Catherine is depressed, and the fact that there is no news from Bath does not raise her spirits; on the tenth day they are further lowered when she receives James's letter saying that the engagement between himself and Isabella is off. He is very sorry for himself, and Catherine is hurt and bitterly disappointed in her friend. Next General Tilney, knowing that Henry has to go to Woodston for a parish meeting, proposes that they all visit him there the following week. This visit passes off delightfully, particularly for Catherine, and the day after they get back Catherine receives Isabella's letter which indicates that she wishes to be engaged to James again (indeed she affects to believe that she still is) and asking Catherine to write to him on her behalf. She affects too to dislike Captain Tilney, who has obviously turned his amorous attentions in another direction.

Meanwhile General Tilney goes to London for a week, and Henry is away at Woodston when the General returns. Without any explanation he summarily instructs Eleanor that Catherine must leave the Abbey, and she leaves early next morning, to return unescorted and on borrowed money to her parents in Fullerton; they, and the Allens who have returned from Bath, hear Catherine's story and are offended, but before Catherine can brood for too long Henry arrives, walks with her to see the Allens, proposes to her and is joyfully accepted. Henry then unravels to Catherine the mystery of his father's sudden change of attitude towards her: the same John Thorpe, piqued at his own and his sister Isabella's lack of success with Catherine and James, has now told the General that the Morlands are wretchedly poor. This is of course as untrue as his earlier assertion of their great wealth.

The Morlands cannot accede to the actual marriage until the General's approval has been obtained. When Eleanor makes a fortunate marriage she persuades her father to pardon Henry, and he graciously gives his consent.

Chronologically the plot or action of the novel occupies about eleven weeks, as Chapman convincingly demonstrates in his appendix on the Chronology of *Northanger Abbey* in Volume 5 of *The Novels of Jane Austen*, and the action would appear to take place in 1798 despite the subsequent revisions of the book, which was originally called *Susan*.

Chapter summaries, critical commentaries, textual notes and revision questions

Chapter 1

The ironic tone which characterizes so much of Jane Austen's work is immediately apparent in the description of Catherine, her childhood, her family and her background and all the formative influences that have established her as being 'in training for a heroine'. There are many sly digs at other novelists and their presentation and conception of heroines. Catherine has been a tomboy, and her capabilities are certainly unexceptional; essentially, she is a normal girl, part of whose education has been to study the 'right' authors. But alas, so far she has not met an eligible young man, yet her prospects of doing so appear to change when her neighbours Mr and Mrs Allen invite her to go to Bath with them for a stay of some weeks.

Commentary

The opening is a gloriously ironic snipe at the conventional valuation of romantic heroines. Jane Austen is poking fun at the Gothic novels (see the section on this earlier). These provide the main object of both satire and irony in *Northanger Abbey*. By mocking the sensational Jane Austen is indicating that *her* novel is rooted in reality. There is a considered emphasis on Catherine, whose ordinariness and normality are underlined by the fact that she is essentially lovable. She is not very bright, has no capacity for music or art (unlike most heroines), though she delights in being called 'pretty' as she matures. The author's use of her own voice in perspective on her heroine is seen to good effect – 'But from fifteen to seventeen she was in training for a heroine' (p.23) that is, she reads the right books expected of her. The quotations provided by the author extend the tone of mockery, for she is subtly contrasting the world of literature with the world of reality. We note the influence of the major 18th-century writers and Shakespeare on Jane Austen. The mockery is sustained by reference to Catherine's supposed inadequacies, and the chapter ends with an ironic comment on the fortuitous circumstance of the heroine receiving an invitation to Bath where she may be expected to meet with adventure. 'Mr and Mrs Morland were all complaisance, and Catherine all happiness' (p.24), a good example of the admirable balance of Jane Austen's style.

born to be an heroine Note the irony at once – Jane Austen is intent on mocking the conventional attitudes towards the heroines of fiction, particularly in Gothic novels.
Richard See note, p.231, in the Pan edition – a reference to an Austen family joke.
independence . . . livings He had money of his own in addition to the income received from the two parishes in which he officiated as a clergyman.
locking up his daughters i.e. playing the heavy father – or the evil father of the Gothic romances.
unpropitious for heroism i.e. (Catherine) was unpromising material to be outstanding or beautiful – the stuff of which heroines are made.
propensities Leanings towards, interests.
'Beggar's Petition' See note, p.231, in Pan edition – obviously a moral tale, instructive of Christianity for the young.
'The Mare and Many Friends' One of the *Fables* of the writer John Gay (1685–1732) published in 1727. (He was, of course, the author of *The Beggar's Opera*, 1728.)
spinnet Small wing-shaped harpsichord with one string to each note. (Usually spelt 'spinet'.)
profligacy Ironic way of putting it – it means 'licentiousness', and Catherine is very far from this.
mending i.e. improving.
consequence i.e. was becoming rounded, filling out.
lying-in i.e. childbirth.
baseball Game like rounders with stick and ball.
in training for a heroine Again the irony, almost as if 'heroine' is a professional occupation.
to supply their memories . . . serviceable A playful dig at false education, which supplies quotation but no real knowledge.
Pope Alexander Pope (1688–1744) the great Augustan poet admired by Jane Austen. The line quoted is from his 'To The Memory of An Unfortunate Lady'.
Gray Thomas Gray (1716–71). The lines are from the celebrated *Elegy Written in a Country Churchyard*, and the misquotation is that the original reads 'sweetness', not 'fragrance'.
Thomson James Thomson (1700–48) author of *The Seasons*, the lines here being a slight misquotation from *Spring*.
Shakespeare (1564–1616), the first quotation being from *Othello*, Act III, Scene 3 (confirmation should be in the plural); the second from *Measure for Measure*, Act III, Scene 1, with 'feel' being 'finds' in the original; the third is an accurate quotation from *Twelfth Night*, Act II, Scene 4.
sonnets Celebrated in the Elizabethan period in particular, poems of

fourteen lines, generally in adoration of the writer's mistress; here Jane Austen is mocking the romantic convention of writing poetic effusions.

reared and supported a boy . . . origin was unknown Again mockery of the 18th-century novelists who formed their heroes from the abandoned child (like Fielding's *The History of Tom Jones; a Foundling*.)

Bath In the eighteenth and nineteenth centuries, the greatest centre of fashion and culture outside London, famous too for its architecture and the curative powers of its waters.

Chapter 2

Catherine takes leave of her family, and shortly afterwards arrives at Bath. There follows a detailed and delightfully ironic description of Mrs Allen, a foolish woman who is only interested in dress. Catherine and Mrs Allen go to the ballroom but Catherine is not asked to dance; they squeeze out through the throng in search of tea, with Catherine feeling uncomfortable that they do not know anybody. When the dancing is over, Mr Allen rejoins them and Catherine is now reduced to yawning – though as they leave she hears two gentlemen refer to her as 'a pretty girl'.

Commentary

Before the running irony continues, there is a plain assertion of Catherine's worth ('her heart was affectionate, her disposition cheerful and open, without conceit or affectation of any kind' p.25). Mrs Morland is certainly not the mother in a Gothic novel, for her fears for Catherine are not concerned with the attentions of men; rather she is apprehensive that Catherine may catch cold. It is quite obvious that Jane Austen is intent on displaying 'the common feelings of common life' (p.26). Even the journey to Bath is subject to mockery, since nothing happens! The all-encompassing irony focuses on Mrs Allen, who 'had neither beauty, genius, accomplishment, nor manner' (p.27) and who is grossly insensitive except with regard to her dress. The atmosphere in the ballroom is well conveyed as Mrs Allen makes her way complacently through the crush. Catherine's spirit is roused by the boring repetitions of Mrs Allen, her sensitivity by her feeling out of things. Note the naturalness of the dialogue between Mrs Allen and Catherine. Catherine is so natural indeed that she cannot suppress a yawn, but although she is not called 'a divinity' (p.30) she at least has a boost to her morale by the remark on her prettiness. Naturally she feels that the evening has been much better than it was in reality because of this.

about as ignorant and uninformed . . . usually is Occasionally, as here, there is an ironic sting at the end of a paragraph, when the author employs her own voice.
their parting conference in her closet The latter would be a small room off the main bedroom – but note the inflated language, again in mockery of the style and assumptions of the Gothic novelists.
machinations Cunning plans.
overturn i.e. of the coach or carriage in which they were travelling.
clogs i.e. wooden-soled overshoes for walking on wet ground.
a last volume Novels were published in three or four volumes, and in Gothic novels the climax or the unravelling of all the mysteries was naturally reserved for the final one.
chaperon i.e. companion who acts as protector or protectress; often spelt 'chaperone'.
Upper Rooms See note in Pan edition, p.232.
The season was full i.e. at its peak.
protegée One to whom another person is protector or patron.
high feathers i.e. on the head-dresses.
with perfect serenity Again note the irony, which implies that only what relates to dress touches Mrs Allen's feelings.
started with rapturous wonder Here Jane Austen is satirizing the kind of exaggerated phrasing used by the Gothic novelists to suggest sudden romantic attraction.
a divinity i.e. a goddess.
a true quality heroine . . . fifteen sonnets Note the irony again.
her chair i.e. a sedan chair, borne by two men.

Chapter 3

The daily ritual of shopping and visits described. Catherine is introduced to Henry Tilney, who has a satirical style of his own, sending up the way people 'do' Bath, even sending himself up too. He also waxes satirical about young girls who commit everything of the day's events to their journals or to letter-writing. Henry holds up well, too, in conversation with Mrs Allen when she appears, and affects a great interest in and knowledge of dress, thus pressing his satire on the class of fashionable men who would be expected to have just such interests. Henry himself is eminently respectable, being a clergyman from Gloucestershire.

Commentary

Henry Tilney's satirical nature has been indicated above. It is reinforced by the author's account of Mrs Allen and Catherine 'looking at everybody and speaking to no one' (p.31). Note the detailed description of Henry Tilney and the latter's whimsical humour, as well as the naturalness of the dialogue. Henry has a great capacity to laugh at himself. His constant reference to Catherine keeping a journal is a continuation of the mockery of the Gothic novel, where heroines would confide all their thoughts to their diaries of events. Henry is also sharp in his attack on women's letters, but his best moments are seen in his apparent deference to Mrs Allen and his affectation of an interest in dress. He is vivacious and entertaining.

the Pump-room A famous building in Bath where the medicinal waters were drunk. It was also a society meeting-place.
The master of the ceremonies James King, Master of Ceremonies from 1785 to 1805 (see note in Pan edition p.232).
in your journal Young ladies – and particularly heroines! – committed their secrets to their diaries ('journals') or to their friends by letter.
a queer, half-witted man Note Henry's own humour re himself.
A general deficiency This embraces the whole of what good letter-writing should *not* consist of.
cravats Neckcloths, fashionably worn at the time.
a prodigious bargain 'Prodigious' is one of the non-words of the time, like 'nice', which is elaborated on later. It is the fashionable cliché word for 'good', equivalent today to 'super', 'great' or 'tremendous'.
discourse Conversation.
before the gentleman's love is declared See note, Pan edition, p.232 – and note too that Jane Austen is mocking Richardson's views.

Chapter 4

Mrs Allen meets an old school friend, Mrs Thorpe. The latter gives an account of her family, and then the Misses Thorpe arrive and are introduced. Catherine learns that they know her brother James, who is at Oxford. Isabella Thorpe, four years older than Catherine, dominates the conversation, and of course the girls immediately become friends. The author in her own voice gives a brief account of the family in order to 'supersede' a much more lengthy one from Mrs Thorpe.

Commentary

Catherine's excitement at the thought of seeing Henry Tilney is conveyed, as well as the anticlimax when she doesn't. The meeting of Mrs Thorpe and Mrs Allen is attended by the usual irony ('they had been contented to know nothing of each other for the last fifteen years' (p.36)) which also notes that neither listens to the other but just keeps talking regardless. Mrs Allen, with less to retail, falls back naturally on the superiority of her own dress. Isabella Thorpe is overpowering, but not so to the lonely Catherine – 'Friendship is certainly the finest balm for the pangs of disappointed love' (p.38). Isabella is the beauty of the family, and Catherine is all gratitude for her attentions. The chapter ends with another ironic aside by the author of how she might have told Mrs Thorpe's story according to the Gothic convention, but prefers instead to state facts.

complaisance Politeness, obligingness.
expatiated i.e. enlarged upon.
Merchant-Taylors' A famous public school.
pelisse A woman's mantle reaching to the ankles; it has armholes or sleeves.
amity Friendship.
Friendship is certainly the finest balm Another choice example of wisdom and the author's ability to express it in finely-balanced and economical prose.
quizzes Ridiculous people; see note Pan editon, p.232.
Tunbridge A popular watering place on the borders of Kent and Sussex.
This brief account Note that Jane Austen frequently employs her own voice in moral commentary, or in appraisal of her heroine or of life. The omniscient author is very much part of 18th- and 19th-century fiction, but Jane Austen, although she digresses at times, generally facilitates rather than impedes the narrative flow.
supersede Take the place of.

Chapter 5

Catherine sees the Thorpes after divine service the next day, but looks in vain for Henry Tilney. Catherine confides in Isabella about him, and the friendship between the two girls progresses quickly and warmly, though perhaps superficially. The chapter closes with the author addressing the reader in her own voice again, this time in an eloquent defence of the novel, which is 'only some work in which the greatest powers of the mind are displayed, in which the most thorough knowledge of human nature, the happiest delineation of its varieties, the liveliest effusions of wit and humour, are conveyed to the world in the best-chosen language'.

Commentary

Apart from the authorial commentary quoted above, there is much emphasis in this chapter on the naive eagerness of Catherine to see Henry Tilney. It is an endearing and natural wish, and contrasts effectively with the essentially superficial nature of her relationship with Isabella – though at this stage Catherine does not realize this. In fact she does not respond, because she is too innocent, to Isabella's obvious invitation to hear her confidences. We note that Mrs Thorpe and Mrs Allen talk only on their own subjects. The irony of the fast-developing friendship between Catherine and Isabella gives way to the eloquent defence of the novel mentioned above. *Northanger Abbey* is an early novel, and in it Jane Austen gives full rein to her own view of the importance of the novel as an art form. This slows the narrative, but is direct evidence of her seriousness of intention in the moral and aesthetic sense.

insupportable Intolerable; it was too crowded.
dressed or undressed i.e. formal or informal.
curricle-drivers Those of light two-wheeled carriages, usually having two horses abreast.
the Pump-room book It recorded the names of visitors.
finesse Artfulness, cunning, strategy.
delicate raillery i.e. subtle innuendo or mockery.
the set i.e. taking positions in the dance opposite partners.
Yes, novels There follows a spirited and eloquent defence of the novel, which was not considered as a serious art form at the time.
Reviewers The word begins with a capital because the monthly reviews carried considerable weight and could make or break the reputation of an author.
History of England Heavy irony, since there were many editions for the edification of the young.
Milton (1608–74), the major poet of the seventeenth century, author of *Paradise Lost, Samson Agonistes* and *Lycidas* among other major works.
Pope See note p.23.
Prior The minor poet Matthew Prior (1664–1721).
Spectator The celebrated publication in the reign of Queen Anne under

the editorship of Joseph Addison and Sir Richard Steele; the most famous of its essays contain the much-loved character of Sir Roger de Coverley.

Sterne Laurence Sterne (1713–68), the English humorist and somewhat unconventional novelist, author of *Tristram Shandy* and *A Sentimental Journey*.

Cecilia* or *Camilla Both by Fanny Burney (Madame D'Arblay, 1752–1840). They are novels of fashionable life.

Belinda This was by Maria Edgeworth (1766–1849), and dealt with Irish life.

Chapter 6

This records a conversation about Gothic novels between Catherine and Isabella, and is largely satirical in tone and intention. Isabella's conversation confirms that she is a superficial and gossipy character (though Catherine's inexperience means that she cannot see this), and gives hints about her relationship with James, which Catherine does not understand. The girls follow two young men noticed by Isabella, who has affected to think them 'odious'.

Commentary

The author's irony is directed at the nature and quality of the conversation between the two girls. Isabella is seen as silly and affected, Catherine as unspoilt and unsophisticated. The sensational elements of the Gothic novel are dwelt upon, with the impressionability of the girls stressed – 'are you sure they are all horrid?' (p.44). Isabella's comments on Miss Andrews are an index to her own self-conceit. She is completely superficial, flattering Catherine over Mr Tilney, and calling *Sir Charles Grandison* 'an amazing horrid book' (p.45). Isabella affects to know all about men and to deride them, but of course she is intent on attracting them. This she shows in the conversation about the two young men, while she is hypocritically coy about her feelings for James Morland. This provides a delightfully ironic interchange, for Catherine does not know what she is talking about.

coquelicot i.e. orange-red; the colour of the wild poppy.

Udolpho *The Mysteries of Udolpho*, the most celebrated of the Gothic Romances, was published in 1794. It was part of a number of successes achieved by Ann Radcliffe (1764–1823).

the black veil This incident is found in Volume 2, Chapter 6, and the lady involved is Laurentini, not Laurentina.

Castle of Wolfenbach The Pan edition provides the names of the authors of this formidable Gothic list: *Castle of Wolfenbach* by Mrs Parsons (1793), *Clermont* by Regina Roche (1798) *The Mysterious Warning* by Mrs Parsons (1796); *The Necromancer* translated by Peter Teuthold (1794); *The Midnight Bell* (1798); *The Orphans of the Rhine* by Mrs Eleanor Sleath (1798); *Horrid Mysteries* translated from the German by Peter Will (1796).

Miss Andrews There is even something ironic in the choice of name, for Pamela Andrews was the name of Richardson's moral heroine in *Pamela* (1741), satirized by Fielding as having an equally moral brother in *Joseph Andrews* (1742).

netting A fashionable occupation of the time, rather like crochet.

Sir Charles Grandison Published in 1753–4, Richardson's final novel (1689–1761), with a hero – largely unsympathetic – who epitomizes moral rectitude.

the arrivals i.e. the book recording all the names of those who had arrived to stay in Bath. (See note, Pan edition, p.233).

Chapter 7

Isabella and Catherine meet James Morland and John Thorpe, driving a gig. John Thorpe proves to be a loud and boastful young man talking about his horse and gig, exaggerating all the time. He further reveals his ignorance when they discuss (if that is the word) Gothic novels. His manners are crude, but James Morland thinks well of him, and tells Catherine how glad he is to see that she is friendly with Isabella. Catherine later continues her reading of *The Mysteries of Udolpho*.

Commentary

Note that Jane Austen manages to convey very successfully the sense of place, of actually knowing Bath in some detail. The failure to make contact with the two young men frustrates Isabella, but this gives way to her overt flirtation with James Morland. Thorpe is both arrogant and inaccurate, and we note the family likeness between Catherine and her brother, and between Thorpe and Isabella. Thorpe is all mouth and, as far as we can gather, no judgement. Isabella, happy in James's company, sees the two young men again but 'looked back at them only three times' (p.50), the author's tone sufficiently castigating her for doing so. Thorpe continues ignorant, his most blatant faux pas concerning the authorship of *Udolpho*. Every time he opens his mouth he is guilty of some unconsidered rubbish. His greeting of his mother is ill-bred, and a delightful irony describes as 'fraternal tenderness' (p.53) his respects to his sisters. We can see when Catherine and James talk that both have been duped by the superficiality of Isabella. There is, however, a charming and sincere exchange of affection between James and Catherine.

devoirs Respects; (literally 'duties' from the French).
amends i.e. attentions.
Tetbury A cotswold town some 35km (22 miles) from Bath by road – but see Pan note, p.233.
Serape i.e. moving his foot backwards as he bows to her.
forehand See note in Pan edition which refers to the front part of the horse.
gig Light, two-wheeled one-horse carriage.
Christ-church i.e. the Oxford college of that name.
Magdalen Bridge The main Oxford bridge, alongside Magdalen College, Oxford.
closed i.e. reached an agreement with.
Oriel An Oxford college.
Tom Jones Picaresque novel by Henry Fielding (1707–54), generally considered to be his masterpiece. It was published in 1749.
The Monk By Mathew Gregory Lewis (1796). A particularly vicious horror novel. (See also Olivia Manning's Pan note, p.233).
Mrs Radcliffe's See note on *Udolpho*, p.29, and Section on the Gothic novel, beginning p.13.
she who married the French emigrant i.e. Fanny Burney, Madame D'Arblay. (See note p.29).
Camilla See note p.29.
an old man's playing at see-saw . . . In chapters 3 and 4 of *Camilla*, Book 1.
quiz See Pan note for Chapter 4 on 'quizzes', p.232.
rattle A lightweight, talkative person.
muff and tippet Fur covering for hands, and small fur cape.

Chapter 8

The dance at the Upper Rooms and what ensued are described in this chapter. Isabella, having said she will not dance and thus leave Catherine alone, of course does so. Mrs Hughes and Miss Tilney however, accompanied by Henry, appear, and Henry asks Catherine to dance. Afterwards Isabella returns, again dances with James (having vowed she will not); then Catherine refuses to dance with John Thorpe, who has been away from the group anyway, but she is a little annoyed that she has missed Mr Tilney, who is now dancing with someone else.

Commentary

Isabella displays her fickleness at the outset, standing out for three minutes before succumbing to the need to dance. Catherine on her own – she has been deserted by John Thorpe – proves by her stoicism that she has the true spirit of the heroine. Catherine's sight of her acquaintance Henry Tilney occasions more irony, since she guesses that the lady on his arm is his sister and not a romantic attachment. When Mr Tilney asks her to dance Catherine is mortified, since she has been deserted by John Thorpe yet is still obliged out of etiquette to refuse the offer of the partner she most wants – Henry. She puts up bravely with Thorpe's insensitive conversation, having some compensation in the fact that immediately after that dance she meets Miss Tilney. Her wish to get to know her is frustrated by the ever-demanding Isabella, who contradicts herself a few times, and sees herself always as the centre of attraction. Catherine has spirit enough to reject John Thorpe's condescension of dancing with her, but she really longs to see more of Mr Tilney.

in a bustle i.e. in a chatter, gossiping about us because of our unconventional behaviour.

Chapter 9

John Thorpe, his sister and James arrive, intent on driving, possibly to Claverton Down; Catherine is expected to join them. She does so, and finds herself thoroughly bored by the loudness and outrageousness of Thorpe, for none of his conversation stands up to rational consideration. While they are away, Mrs Allen meets Miss Tilney and Mrs Hughes, and the latter tells Mrs Allen about the Tilneys, information which is naturally relayed to Catherine on her return.

Commentary

We are given a keen insight into Catherine's character by her reactions – unhappiness, hunger, deep sleep, which follow a natural rather than an extraordinary pattern. She organizes herself admirably the following morning despite the interruptions of Mrs Allen. Thorpe's ill-mannered brusqueness on his arrival puts Catherine out, but she responds good-naturedly, and has the pleasure of hearing Isabella say that she dotes on her. There is some anti-climax in the surprisingly good behaviour of Thorpe's horses, but his interrogation of Catherine about Mr Allen being rich has an important plot function (apart from stressing Thorpe's complete lack of breeding) in that it prepares us for the wrong-headed reaction of General Tilney later to Catherine's supposed wealth. At least when there is a discussion of heavy drinking Catherine is left with the happy impression that her brother is something of a sober man. But now she is worried by the thought that James's gig will break down, a thought encouraged by the insensitive John Thorpe. Catherine hears the story – and it is certainly fiction – of all John Thorpe's doings. She now begins to have doubts, though she 'bore with the effusions of his endless conceit' (p.69). Isabella cannot bear to lose Catherine when they return, but Catherine is filled with chagrin when she realizes that Mrs Thorpe and Mrs Allen have seen the Tilneys. We note that whereas Catherine's questioning of Mrs Allen is honest and naive, John Thorpe's questioning of Catherine earlier was filled (perhaps) with cunning intent.

from habitude very little incommoded i.e. Catherine was so used to Mrs Allen's non-stop comments that they no longer bothered her.
Claverton Down A short ride, 3km–5km (2–3 miles) from Bath.
take the rest i.e. be restive, difficult to manage.
gouty Having gout: inflammation of a joint, particularly of the big toe – commonly associated with drinking too much but in fact due to a faulty diet, and perhaps a hereditary factor.
bottle-a-day i.e. of wine.
in liquor i.e. drunk.
overset i.e. turned over – drunk, incapable.
equipage i.e. coach and horses.
the best goer i.e. having the most stamina, a good performer.
tittuppy i.e. lively and frisky, but here the innuendo is that it is insecure, falling to pieces, jumping about and not capable of keeping to the road.
roll i.e. a tumble.
a rattle See note p.31.
intelligence i.e. information of importance.

Chapter 10

Morlands and Thorpes and Allens go to the theatre, but Catherine does not see the Tilneys there. Next morning she hopes to see them at the Pump-room; to her delight she meets Miss Tilney and has a long talk with her. She learns that Henry has gone for a ride with his father that morning, but Miss Tilney is astute enough to realize the state of Catherine's feelings (unbeknown to herself) about Henry. The next evening Catherine goes to the cotillion ball, and Henry asks her to dance, though the ill-bred John Thorpe claims her. She dances and talks with Henry, though, and has a delightful exchange with him. Later she notices that she is being watched, and learns from Henry that the gentleman concerned is his father.

Commentary

Isabella's rattling on is all designed to make Catherine aware that she (Isabella) and James were destined for one another. Catherine is obtuse, but not deliberately so, and this has the effect of diminishing Isabella's ploy. The next morning Catherine feels sensitive because James and Isabella seem to be engrossed with each other and have no place for her. She meets Miss Tilney, and we note the frankness of the exchanges between them (the contrast is with Isabella), their commonplaces redolent of 'simplicity and truth, and without personal conceit' (p.73). Catherine unconsciously reveals her feelings for Henry to Miss Tilney. Later she thinks about dress, and draws down upon herself some censure from her creator. The change in Catherine is duly noted – she wants to avoid seeing John Thorpe on Thursday evening. She dances with Henry, and their interchange is interrupted by John Thorpe; the contrast in breeding and refinement is developed. Henry himself draws a witty contrast between dancing and marriage; it is a measure of his intelligent, cultivated, sophisticated nature. Another contrast explored is that between Bath and country life, and Catherine's naiveté shows to advantage. Some dramatic effect is achieved by the focus on General Tilney.

cotillion The name for several dances.
Dress is at all times a frivolous distinction Again the moral tone is implicit in the comment.
tamboured muslin Embroidered muslin.
mull . . . jackonet Mull is a thin plain muslin; 'jackonet' (spelt 'jaconet' today) is a heavier cotton fabric.
her engagement to Thorpe This of course means her promise to dance with him – *not* to marry him.

emblem i.e. symbolic of, equivalent to.
purvey i.e. provide, supply.
the bottom of the set i.e. the end of the groups of dancers, seen in terms of formation.

Revision questions on Chapters 1–10

1 What are the main objects of Jane Austen's irony in the first few chapters of *Northanger Abbey*?

2 Do you find Catherine Morland endearing or dull?

3 What evidence is there in these early chapters that Jane Austen is seriously interested in the novel as an art form?

4 What effect does either Henry Tilney or John Thorpe have on Catherine?

5 Write an essay on the nature of the dialogue and its effects so far on one or two of the characters.

Chapter 11

Catherine has arranged to go for a walk with Miss Tilney the next morning, but the weather threatens to be none too favourable. Thorpe and Isabella and Catherine's brother James again importune her to go for a drive to Bristol with them; when Catherine sticks to her hope that the Tilneys will turn up, they tempt her with a visit to Blaize Castle. On this she agrees to go, but as they are leaving, or rather when they have gone a little way, she sees Henry and Miss Tilney. Thorpe is too obstinate and pig-headed to stop, but the party never get to Blaize Castle, and are forced to turn back. When she arrives home, Catherine learns that a lady and gentleman have called on her, but have left no card. She and the others spend the evening at the Thorpe's, playing cards.

Commentary

There is the usual humour at the expense of Mrs Allen, and the generation of some tension over the rain. Catherine's opposition to the drive – despite the temptation of Blaize Castle – is well conveyed, as is the distortion of John and Isabella. There is a fine dramatic moment when Catherine sees the Tilneys walking and John Thorpe refuses to stop. The prospect of Blaize Castle is a

Gothic one, Catherine indulges her imagination with the horrors to be, and it is more than an anti-climax when they turn back. An important plot emphasis which Catherine does not understand is seen in John Thorpe's reference to people who 'rolled in money', for he is to tell the General (Tilney) that Catherine is an heiress. The author closes the chapter on a worried Catherine – 'And now I may dismiss my heroine to the sleepless couch . . .' (p.89). The irony here is that Catherine is suffering but Austen is mocking the synthetic heroines of horror novels in unreal situations, who are supposed to suffer extravagantly.

take a chair i.e. a sedan chair.
poor St Aubin The father of the heroine, he dies in *The Mysteries of Udolpho*. His name is really St Aubert.
Clifton Clifton was then a village on the river Avon near Bristol – now one of its fashionable suburbs.
Kingsweston A hamlet near Bristol.
croaking i.e. anticipating evil.
Blaize Castle . . . The oldest in the kingdom Another bit of irony; Blaize Castle was built in the eighteenth century.
Wick Rocks In a deep glen about 14km (9 miles) west of Bristol.
counterpoise i.e. balance, in this case an attractive or compensatory one (after her disappointment over the Tilneys).
Keynsham A village almost midway on the road between Bath and Bristol.
broken-winded jade's i.e. useless or run-down horse (a derogatory expression).
a pool of commerce A card game, which features exchange and barter – rather like Isabella, who 'exchanges' one suitor for another but ultimately loses both.

Chapter 12

Catherine goes to visit Miss Tilney, but receives a rebuff when the servant tells her she is not at home. Catherine, however, looks back and sees Miss Tilney leaving the house with her father. Some time later she sees Henry Tilney at the theatre, and pours out her apologies to him for not having waited for him and his sister on that fateful morning. It is arranged that they will take another walk to replace the one they have missed. Catherine notices that John Thorpe is talking to General Tilney; and later Thorpe tells her that the General thinks her the finest girl in Bath.

Commentary

Catherine's visit is fraught with tension, and we share her anguish at the rebuff by Miss Tilney. The state of her feelings for Henry Tilney is revealed later in the evening when he and his father enter the theatre at the beginning of the final act of the play. When Henry comes round to see Catherine afterwards he cannot resist the spontaneous honesty of her assertion that she had not wanted to go on the drive with John Thorpe and the others the previous day. Thorpe's chat with General Tilney – leaving aside more evidence of his boasting – is important to the plot, for he is obviously telling the General of Catherine's supposed 'wealth'. Catherine's own morale is boosted by the knowledge that General Tilney has pronounced her to be a fine girl, but she has to endure the boorish flattery of John Thorpe as well.

the Bedford Probably refers to the coffee-house of that name in Covent Garden, London.
a little touch A game.

Chapter 13

Again the idea of the Clifton scheme comes up, and Catherine annoys her brother and more particularly the Thorpes by saying that she is engaged to go out with Miss Tilney and therefore cannot accompany them. Thorpe then takes it upon himself to go and see Miss Tilney to get Catherine released from her commitment, but when he returns Catherine is furious and goes straight to the Tilneys herself. She spends the rest of the day with the Tilneys, at the General's invitation, and returns to Pulteney Street to find that in any case the Allens disapprove of the idea of her driving away with Mr Thorpe. She thinks of writing to Isabella, but in the end does not do so.

Commentary

The chapter opens with an ironic comment on the 'pangs' of the seventh day, the previous six having been described. Catherine demonstrates her growing independence by refusing to take part in the Clifton scheme, in which her brother James is a dupe. Catherine is maturing, and refuses to be bullied. Note that as usual Isabella speaks in excessive terms – Catherine is her dearest, sweetest, beloved – but when this fails to work she accuses her of a preference for Miss Tilney. This is moral blackmail, and it is reinforced by the weakness of James, who now openly sides against his sister. Catherine is injured but firm, and her reaction to John Thorpe's insensitive visit to Miss Tilney is an uncompromising one. We admire Catherine, who surely represents moral rightness of attitude and decision in this and other instances. She is certainly beginning to see through Isabella. She displays great courage and spirit. She also throws dignity to the winds. Her sincerity shines through with the Tilneys. There is an ominous forecast of the General's future behaviour in his choosing to blame his servant. Catherine is merely delighted by the extent of his attentions to her. But she has something of a conscience, and *nearly* writes to Isabella.

Chapter 14

The Tilneys call at the appointed time, and on their walk they discuss *The Mysteries of Udolpho.* Henry acknowledges that he reads novels of this kind, but Miss Tilney holds forth on the merits of history. Thereafter Catherine learns much of drawing and perspective from the informed conversation of her companions. Catherine later reverts to the topic of Gothic novels, saying that a new one will shortly be published in London; then Henry gives his own fictitious account of what it will consist of. Henry continues his delightfully informed banter, and when Catherine arrives back she learns that Maria, one of the Thorpe sisters, has taken her place on the drive to Clifton.

Commentary

At first apprehensive of another row, Catherine soon gives herself up to enjoyment of the walk with the Tilneys. Henry Tilney is used by the author for another defence of the novel as a worthwhile art form. In fact there is some praise for the qualities of suspense in *The Mysteries of Udolpho.* Henry again shows his wit in the niceties of language, playing particularly on the imprecise use of the word 'nice' for example. Catherine stresses the quality of the imagination, while the debate on history is civilized, cultured and intelligent conversation, something lacking in the oaths and boasting of John Thorpe and the effusions of his sister Isabella.

Catherine feelingly recalls the nature of instruction of the young as being a form of torment. Catherine herself however receives instruction in the form of sketching and perspective from her delightful companions, though when Henry turns to politics his creator ironically observes that 'from politics, it was an easy step to silence' (p.109). There is a wonderful slice of humour when Catherine announces that something terrible is to come out shortly in London, and Henry correctly interprets this for his bewildered sister by saying that it is a reference to a Gothic novel. He continues to tease Catherine lightly, but such is her capacity for enjoyment in his company that she has a thoroughly happy day, even generously wishing that all the Thorpe girls could have gone on the trip to Clifton with their brother and sister.

Julias and Louisas i.e. heroines of Gothic novels.
Emily herself left poor Valancourt The latter is the hero of *The Mysteries of Udolpho*, separated from the heroine Emily.
sampler A piece of embroidery.
Johnson and Blair References to Dr Johnson's Dictionary of 1755 and Blair's *Lectures on Rhetoric* (1783).
Mr Hume or Mr Robertson The first the author of the *History of England* (1754–62), the second author of *The History of Scotland* (1759).
Caractacus, Agricola, or Alfred the Great The first was a British chief, King of the Silures, who put up a brave fight against the Romans, but was eventually captured and carried off in triumph to Rome. The Emperor Claudius was so impressed by his dignity and his general demeanour that he had him and his companions set free. *Agricola* was the Roman general who conquered Great Britain in AD 80 but was later recalled to Rome and retired to private life (AD 37–93). *Alfred the Great* was the King of the West Saxons (AD 849–901); he was a man of letters and a great leader and administrator, virtually establishing the English fleet.
a sister author A reference to Fanny Burney and *Camilla*. The Pan notes by Olivia Manning (p.235) identify the 'beautiful girl' as Indiana in *Camilla*.
three duodecimo volumes The common mode of publication. Duodecimo is one-twelfth of a printing sheet, so these are small volumes.
two tombstones and a lantern Symbolic of death and perhaps secret burial, or even body-snatching!
St George's Fields Where the Gordon Riots occurred in 1780.
the Tower i.e. of London.

Chapter 15

Early the next day Catherine receives a note from Isabella, and when she sees Catherine she confides to her her love for James – something she has been hinting at obstinately ever since they met, but which the guileless Catherine hasn't noticed. Isabella describes her own sufferings and uncertainties in the cause of love; naturally she longs for the consent of the Morland parents, and when James sends the letter saying he has obtained it, all is joy. After this John Thorpe comes to see Catherine. In his clumsy way he comes somewhere near to a proposal of marriage to Catherine, but not near enough for her to notice it! And when she gives the news of James and Isabella to Mr and Mrs Allen, she finds that they have been expecting it all along.

Commentary

There is a fine irony in the fact that the drive the previous day did not go to Blaize Castle, so Catherine has missed nothing. There is something humorous about Catherine's 'wondering ignorance' before Isabella gives her the news of her love for James. It must be observed that there is little to suggest that it is sincere. Catherine is rightly taken aback by Isabella saying that she – Catherine – will be more to her than her own sisters. Isabella's recollections of her falling in love consist more of remembering what she (and Miss Andrews) wore, a clear indication of her shallowness. There is drama as we wait for the news of James's visit to get his parents' consent. There are subtle indications throughout the chapter that Isabella considers that James is rich. She delights in affecting to like the country, already thinks of settling near Richmond, plans her wedding gown and takes a repetitive farewell of James which comes to farce. Isabella is neurotic enough to be almost genuinely in a state of distress before the news arrives, and we note Catherine's considerateness towards her. When the good news does arrive Isabella is able to indulge her fantasy of the future. There is something at once comic and pathetic in John Thorpe's near proposal to Catherine. There is also an eye to the main chance, since he believes that she has or will have money. He retires with some complacency.

bespoke i.e. ordered.
purses and spars The latter are probably ornaments (see Pan note, p. 235).

sarsenet A fine soft silk.
Richmond Remember that the Thorpes come from Putney; Richmond, relatively nearby in Surrey, would be a rather superior country place, having beautiful riverside scenery.
no skulker i.e. did not hold back from, he did not hide his joy.
tickets i.e. visiting cards. (Her married name would be on them.)
hoop rings on her finger i.e. to show her married status.

Chapter 16

Catherine's visit to the Tilneys in Milsom Street is described. Afterwards she is not too pleased, and when she tells Isabella, the latter puts it down to the pride of the family. They see the Tilneys, now joined by the elder brother Captain Tilney that evening. Captain Tilney wishes to dance with Isabella, and the latter changes her mind and gives him that pleasure. The flirtation, which Isabella would be the first to deny, has begun between the two. But the next day the letter arrives detailing Mr Morland's generous treatment – a living of £400 per annum for James when he is married to Isabella. The Thorpes are disconcerted by what they consider to be the smallness of the amount, though Isabella turns this by saying that what she is upset about is the delay in the marriage.

Commentary

Obviously, though Catherine does not quite understand this, Henry and Eleanor are somewhat repressed in their father's company. Again this is important to the plot in view of the fact that the General – unknown at this stage – is a fortune hunter. Isabella quickly reveals her jealousy of the Tilneys, condemning their fickleness though she is to display a like quality herself. Catherine remains uninfluenced by her, another mark of her growing maturity. Captain Tilney is described in some detail, and Jane Austen invents a little Gothic fantasy in which he can have no part, but which contributes to the running humour of the novel. The mutual enjoyment of Catherine and Henry in each other's company is described. Captain Tilney's wish to dance with Isabella is viewed as generosity by Catherine, and Henry generously reveals to her the quality of her own good nature. It is soon put to the test by her seeing Isabella, who had vowed not to dance, smilingly dancing with Captain Tilney. Her later conversation with Catherine underlines her insincerity. The news of Mr

Morland's generosity predictably pricks the bubble of Isabella's fantasy, and Catherine is rightly injured by the insinuations. But she is duped into believing that Isabella is only disappointed at the delay before she can marry – evidence once more of Catherine's trusting nature.

instigator of the three villains Again the satire is directed at the kind of kidnapping scene that forms the staple diet of the Gothic novel.
preparing to give them hands across One of the figures of the dance.

Chapter 17

Catherine learns that the Tilneys are to leave Bath 'By the end of another week!' But there is immediate compensation, for the General invites her to stay with them at Northanger Abbey in Gloucestershire. Mr and Mrs Allen give their approval, and this is echoed when Catherine writes to her parents and gets theirs.

Commentary

Catherine is shocked and surprised when she learns that the Tilneys are to leave Bath. Miss Tilney does her utmost to issue the invitation, but the General times his entrance perfectly to make it with the requisite authority. He also makes it at unpardonable length, but the name 'Northanger' is enough to arouse Catherine's Gothic expectations. Catherine is all ecstasy, but has to endure some of her creator's irony 'Her passion for ancient edifices was next in degree to her passion for Henry Tilney' (p. 132). Her imagination takes off.

Saturday se'night i.e. seven nights from Saturday; we would say 'Saturday week'.
Its long damp passages The whole paragraph is steeped in a mock-Gothic atmosphere in harmony with Catherine's mood – except that Catherine of course takes it all seriously.
the Reformation A reference to the great 16th-century religious movement away from the Church of Rome, which began when Martin Luther defied Pope Leo X. The Church of England was established in 1534, with Henry VIII as its Head.

Chapter 18

Catherine sees Isabella in the Pump-room one morning, and notices that she is continually looking towards the door. Isabella then says that she has heard from her brother John and that he is very much in love with Catherine, and has virtually proposed to her. Catherine is shaken at his wilful interpretation, and also by Isabella's deliberate connivance at it. Captain Tilney arrives and even Catherine, in all her innocence and inexperience, realizes that there is something going on between the Captain and Isabella. The latter pretends to Catherine that she is ignoring the attentions of Captain Tilney.

Commentary

The shallowness, dishonesty and of course the flirtatiousness of Isabella are all exposed in her meeting with Catherine, who innocently supposes her to be looking for James! Isabella insists that John has proposed to her – Catherine – and that Catherine has encouraged him. Note the contrast in the language used by each – Isabella all distortion, Catherine direct truthfulness. Isabella is devious, shown when she admits that 'there are more ways than one of our being sisters' (p. 135). Isabella also unwittingly reveals her own mercenary tendencies. Catherine begins again to see through her 'friend' even before the arrival of Captain Tilney; then, the flirtation which has developed into an affair is all too obvious. But Catherine continues to be generous in her estimate of Isabella, thinking that she is 'unconsciously encouraging him' (Captain Tilney). Catherine's is the balanced view of Thorpe, though she is mainly concerned on her brother's account with regard to Isabella.

But where am I wandering to? R. W. Chapman notes that Isabella is contemplating the fact that they would be sisters if they married Henry and Captain Tilney respectively.

by proxy i.e. on behalf of someone else (Captain Tilney sees Catherine as acting on behalf of her brother).

Chapter 19

Catherine continues to watch Isabella, and finds her something of a changed person. She notices that her brother is made uncomfortable by Isabella's reception of Captain Tilney's attentions. Moreover, Captain Tilney is not going to the Abbey, but is to remain in Bath. Catherine draws Henry's attention to what is going on, but Henry takes the view that the fault lies with Isabella, and that Frederick Tilney's heart is not seriously engaged. When, however, Catherine and the Thorpes spend Catherine's last evening in Pulteney Street, James and Isabella seem happy enough together on this occasion.

Commentary

Catherine continues apprehensive of Isabella's attitude towards Captain Tilney, and indeed of Tilney's ignoring the fact of her engagement, presuming that he knows. Henry assures Catherine that his brother does know, and this increases her anxiety. There is something pathetic in her pleading with Henry to urge Captain Tilney to go away. Catherine is always warm-hearted. Henry's judgement that it is Isabella's fault is a strongly moral one which Catherine cannot deny. Henry in fact talks good sense and wisdom to her about his own brother's shallow nature – and there is an authorial irony playing on the fact that in terms of shallowness Captain Tilney and Isabella deserve each other.

Chapter 20

Catherine goes to Milson Street to breakfast with the Tilneys, but she cannot be altogether at ease with the General. She notices how much there is to eat, and how severe the General is with his children on occasions. The bustle of departure is tedious too, but she later travels in Henry's curricle and has the enjoyment of his companionship and conversation. Henry makes it the occasion for a delightful satire on what Catherine is expecting to find at the Abbey – i.e. a sequence of Gothic mysteries and perhaps horrors. How well he already understands and (kindly) mocks her susceptibilities and the sort of interests Isabella has encouraged. But they arrive at the Abbey too suddenly for her to feel any foreboding. She finds what a contrast the furniture and fittings provide to those created by her imagination.

Commentary

Catherine's sensitivity and her wish to behave properly are the main ingredients of the early part of this chapter. The General is a tyrant, and his reactions to the appearance of Captain Tilney testify to the fact that he is used to being obeyed. He seems to be a thoroughly unpleasant character, although at this stage we probably do not realize how much he thinks there is at stake in his treatment of Catherine. Catherine's speculations about Northanger are pleasantly but ironically mocked: she is worried about propriety when the General invites her to sit with his son after some part of the journey. We note the immediate contrast with John Thorpe's methods of beating and swearing in Henry's controlled moderation. Henry reveals his great affection for Eleanor, and then proceeds to embellish Catherine's own fancy of the Gothic horrors which await them at Northanger. In this he reveals the fertility of his own imagination, though this is in effect a further satire on the Gothic mode. Henry is so good that he almost writes a novel on his own, and he certainly shows a familiarity with the ins and outs of the Gothic plots. Henry indulges the mystical and supernatural elements of such novels to perfection, and despite Catherine's naiveté he finds that he has succeeded in amusing himself at least. Catherine is initially disappointed by the Abbey, but her excitement awakes, and Jane Austen succeeds in conveying a sense of atmosphere and, up to a point, a sense of doom. The General's presence is a brooding one.

a two hours' bait i.e. in order to give the horses refreshment, they stopped.
Nerves fit for sliding panels and tapestry The stand-by 'set' for the drama of the Gothic novel.
toilettes Dressing tables.
Peals of thunder . . . gusts of wind . . . a few drops of blood Henry has quite a talent for Gothic description, and creates the kind of atmosphere calculated to terrify the impressionable girl. But Catherine recovers from this, so that when she reaches the Abbey we are told that 'The breeze had not seemed to waft the sighs of the murdered to her.'
a Rumford See note in Pan edition, p. 235, for the inventor of this modern sloping fireplace.

Revision questions on Chapters 10–20

1 Write an analysis of Catherine's reactions to the various events that contribute to her experience in these chapters.

2 What influence does Catherine's reading have on her when she learns that she is to go to *Northanger Abbey?*

3 What impression have you formed of General Tilney and his relationship with his children?

4 What moral attitude is present in the author's appraisal of the engagement of Isabella and James, and how is this conveyed to the reader?

5 Write an account of the role played by John Thorpe or Captain Tilney in this part of the action.

Chapter 21

Catherine's apartment is described, and though she does not intend to examine it in detail, her interest is taken by observing 'a large high chest, standing back in a deep recess on one side of the fireplace'. She is very curious and tries to open the chest, but is disturbed first by Miss Tilney's maid, and then by Miss Tilney herself. They go down to join the General, who asks her quite a number of questions about Mr Allen and his property. Later Catherine returns to her room, and the atmosphere becomes progressively more eerie and fraught with suspense, all of it emanating from her own heightened imagination. This is further heightened by her seeing an old-fashioned black cabinet corresponding to the one Henry had described. She explores it, and eventually finds a hidden roll of paper. She is about to investigate this when her candle goes out, and 'Darkness impenetrable and immovable filled the room.' This is almost supernaturally followed by a violent gust of wind, and before Catherine falls asleep (after three o'clock), 'Hollow murmurs seemed to creep along the gallery, and more than once her blood was chilled by the sound of distant moans.'

Commentary

Catherine's imagination has been referred to above. The outward normality of the room contrasts with her susceptibility when she sees the chest. We enter her consciousness; the sense of atmosphere is well conveyed, with the interruption of the maid providing a fine anticlimax. Catherine is not lacking in courage, as we see when she opens the lid of the chest – again an anticlimax, although this is followed by embarrassment when Miss Tilney enters. Miss Tilney shows her good manners, but there are hints as to the General's darker side. His questions about Mr Allen imply that Catherine is his heiress, though she does not realize this. The atmosphere takes on greater ominousness because of the storm, and with the discovery of the black cabinet, Catherine's opening it, the discovery of the paper, the going out of the candle, the supposed footsteps, the sleeplessness until three o'clock – all these contribute to the fine comic effects which constitute this Gothic parody.

cypher Secret writing.
toilette i.e. her preparations for going to bed.
so many poor girls . . . obliged to do Catherine is, of course, thinking of hapless Gothic heroines!
Japan Made black and glossy with hard varnish.
celerity Speed.
Darkness impenetrable . . . filled the room Atmosphere, and a Miltonic echo from *Paradise Lost.*
the sound of distant moans Catherine lives in the world of the fiction of the time, so that her imagination transforms anything into menace or the supernatural. At the same time, Jane Austen is playing on the natural human capacity to *imagine* and *fear* more in the darkness of the early hours.

Chapter 22

When Catherine awakes next morning she looks avidly at the manuscript, only to find it is a washing-bill. She is humiliated, and of course anxious to keep her feelings and her discovery from the knowledge of the satirical Henry! Catherine is forced to give her attention to 'the elegance of the breakfast set'. Henry leaves for Woodston, where his living is situated, and the General takes Catherine on a conducted tour of the Abbey, though she would have preferred to be taken by Eleanor. But it is not through the rooms of the Abbey that they go at this juncture, but rather through the grounds, for the General is very proud of their layout and contents. He is very anxious for Catherine to see it all, and is greatly complacent when, in answer to his questions, she reveals that Mrs Allen's place is not nearly so grand or indeed so full of fruit and trees and hot-houses. Then he leaves the girls to continue their talk without him; they enter a particular grove, which Eleanor mentions was her mother's favourite walk. The fact that the General had not been willing to enter the grove leads to a number of questions from Catherine. Her imagination takes flight again, and already she sees the General as a cruel man who has made away with his wife, at worst, or at best treated her badly.

Commentary

An immediate and wonderful sense of anti-climax as Catherine examines the washing-bill, with the effective contrast of daylight reality and darkness imagination and fears. Her sense of shame is great, but then Catherine is so vulnerable that she always has a capacity for suffering. The General is intent on display always, as we see from the breakfast set. The General's comments, however, are rather wasted on Catherine, who is concerned at the departure of Henry. But General Tilney loves the sound of his own voice and continues to indulge it sententiously. When he offers to show Catherine around outside, Miss Tilney, to Catherine's discomfort, is visibly embarrassed. The 'grandeur of the abbey' is described in some detail, while the General's pleasure in Catherine's wonder is somewhat ironic in view of the fact that her own life, unknown to him, is lived in such a small way. He is able to wax complacent, however, when he hears of Mr Allen's horticultural inadequacies. Catherine's imagination – and horror novel apprehensions – are roused again into life by the General's refusing to walk in the grove which was his late wife's private retreat. Catherine also makes the most of the General's rejection of the portrait of his wife.

a washing-bill in her hand We are in the area of burlesque, much loved by Jane Austen, for nothing could be more ridiculous than this reversal of all that Catherine had anticipated. But notice that our sympathy and our interest are always with her.

breeches-ball i.e. a kind of soap for cleaning breeches.

to poultice chestnut mare i.e. treating, with a poultice, a sore place or injury on a horse.

you may in time come to love a rose? Note that Henry is almost forced to be ironic by the naive conversations that Catherine introduces – here, of course, to cover her confusion over her discovery of the washing-bill.

the breakfast set i.e. the crockery used at breakfast.

Staffordshire . . . Dresden . . . Sèvres The first is famous for pottery, the second for china, the third for porcelain. The first is also associated with the designs of Josiah Wedgwood, the second with delicate semi-transparent work, the third with the brilliance of its colours.

The netting-box See note on 'netting', p.30.

a hobby-horse i.e. a particular topic or interest about which he would hold forth at great length.

The pinery Hot-house containing pineapples; to have a pinery was almost a status smbol of superior gardening in the eighteenth century.

succession-houses Where the temperatures are controlled, rising in succession so that plants are moved from a warm house into a warmer one and so on, according to their needs.

Chapter 23

The General returns, ready to escort the girls at last on a tour of the house. He spends much time on the details, indulging his own sense of taste, and explaining everything; Catherine is, if truth be told, a little bored: she is also somewhat confused. The General further conducts them through the offices of which he is so proud. They return to the hall, then go to the gallery and then, to Catherine's excitement, they *almost* go into the room where, says Miss Tilney, her mother died. Later Eleanor promises to show it to her.

Catherine further learns that Eleanor was away from home when her mother died; Catherine is appalled – or, rather, struck with new suspicions of what the General actually did to his wife. That night the General stays up poring over pamphlets, and Catherine immediately leaps to the idea that Mrs Tilney is still alive, hidden in one of the apartments. Consequently she retires full of conjectures about the actual place of the unfortunate woman's incarceration, and plans to explore that very night. But she falls asleep before twelve o'clock.

Commentary

Catherine still reverts to the influences of her reading, speculating Gothic-wise during the tour. The General deepens our impression that he is a conceited, smug, self-satisfied man, intent on display – though here, of course, he thinks that he is hooking a healthy fish. There is a fine contrast between Catherine's boredom and General Tilney's overweening pride. There is a moment of embarrassment for Catherine when the General expresses the wish that she and her family will occupy some of these apartments, but we get the impression that this is a man living beyond his means, a man who employs too many people and sets too much store by ostentation. Catherine's imagination is fed when the General forbids Miss Tilney to show her the staircase and when she learns of Miss Tilney's absence at the time of her mother's death.

closets Small private rooms or cupboards.
pattened i.e. wearing pattens, wooden-soled shoes for safely traversing mud.
dishabille i.e. not dressed properly or formally; from the French *déshabillé*.
worked i.e. engaged in needlework.
Montoni The execrable villain of *The Mysteries of Udolpho*.
boded i.e. foreboded, foretold, indicated.
meetly i.e. fittingly.
revolving these matters i.e. turning them over in her mind.
the guilty scene to be acting i.e. the (imagined) imprisonment of Mrs Tilney.

clock struck twelve... Catherine... asleep At midnight or after all evil things happen, so Catherine, despite her excitement, misses whatever her imagination tells her will be occurring. This is another good example of the author's irony.

Chapter 24

There is no opportunity the next day for an inspection of the 'mysterious apartments', but Catherine notices that the General had erected a monument to the memory of his dead wife. She sees portraits of the dead woman, and the following morning when the General is out of the house persuades Eleanor to show her the rooms; just as they are entering, however, they see the General. She later meets his visitors, and then, summoning her own spirits, determines to go alone to the gallery. At four o'clock she does so, enters the apartment and is amazed at its preserved normality. She is again disturbed, this time by Henry, who enters by another staircase. Henry questions her, then stops, but he describes his mother and the family attendance at her death-bed, so that no further suspicions can possibly exist in Catherine's mind. Henry guesses exactly what her surmises had been, and Catherine, with tears of shame, leaves him.

Commentary

An ironic description of the monument to Mrs Tilney, 'in which every virtue was ascribed to her by the inconsolable husband' (p. 175) only stimulates Catherine's speculations. There is a fine dramatic stroke when Eleanor and Catherine meet the General in the gallery. Later Catherine shows her spirit by deciding to enter the gallery again – though this also shows her obstinacy and the fact that she is obsessed by her sensational reading. Yet the irony which plays over this obsession is a kindly one. Jane Austen superbly builds up the atmosphere which is generated by Catherine's excitement. Henry's sudden appearance provides a dramatic climax to the chapter, and his own revelations about his mother's death and the realism he brings to bear on Catherine's indulgence of wicked thoughts, even crimes, are a salutary experience for that young lady. Even so, we respect Henry's directness; if Catherine, who is so natural, is to live in the real world, she must abandon that world of sensational fantasy in which she has chosen to live.

highly-strained i.e. the sentiments exaggerated, distorted.
a waxen figure might be introduced i.e. into the coffin in place of the real person – another occurrence of Gothic fiction.
inured to Oblivious of, or unaffected by (something), due to having become accustomed to (it).
dimity bed i.e. with a hard-wearing cotton fabric covering.
Bath stove A fireplace with a plate above which would produce the necessary draught.
worked i.e. moved, stirred.
too much wit . . . for detection i.e. too much intelligence to leave anything which would give him away.
only privy i.e. only knowing (her secret was hers alone).
with tears of shame . . . to her own room Superbly economical ending, for in a sense Catherine has reached the end of a particular epoch of her experience.

Chapter 25

Catherine is very upset, though Henry is more assiduous to her than usual. Gradually she comes to terms with her own infatuation with Mrs Radcliffe and her peers, and sees almost for the first time (though her general good sense is never in question) that romance is not reality, and that fiction is not life. She longs for news from Bath, but nothing is forthcoming until the tenth morning, when she receives a letter from her brother James telling her that all is over between Isabella and himself. More than that, he tells her that Isabella and Captain Tilney will become engaged, and hopes that Catherine will have quit Northanger Abbey before Captain Tilney arrives there.

Henry and Eleanor notice her discomfort, the General, deep in his newspaper and his breakfast, does not. She talks to the brother and sister about James's letter, but Henry, though comforting her, waxes satirical about his brother never being capable of committing himself. He also points out to Catherine that she does not really feel as afflicted as she may have thought she would, over the loss of Isabella.

Commentary

Catherine gives herself up to humility, feels that she has ruined herself with Henry, but has not allowed for the enlightenment, tolerance, and genuine feeling of that young man. Most interesting is Catherine's examination of her own Gothic infatuation and the distortions to which it has led, with its final statement that 'she had nothing to do but to forgive herself and be happier than ever' (p. 184). Such is her resilience that she begins to long for a letter from Isabella. Instead – and this is another fine dramatic stroke – she gets one from James. Catherine's feelings for her brother's suffering are genuine, Henry's warmth of sympathy for her complementing them. There is some indication that Henry and Eleanor know how self-seeking their own father is – Catherine praises his generosity to her – and certainly Henry and Eleanor know their own brother. Catherine's transparent honesty makes her acknowledge her own error in judgement over Isabella. She also admits that she doesn't feel that much about losing her friendship.

Most grievously . . . humbled. Most bitterly . . . cry Note the economic effect of the repetition, ironic in view of the fact Catherine is shortly to experience a much greater grief.
abatement i.e. lessening.
Alps and Pyrenees Often chosen as locations for Gothic novels.
rhubarb Generally a purgative, but again the satirical edge of this paragraph is obvious.
memento i.e. reminder.
Putney London suburb, at that time a village, on the Surrey side of the Thames 9.6km (6 miles) from Waterloo, and with a bridge over the river.
Open, candid, artless . . . knowing no disguise Henry, under the pretence of describing Isabella, is very cleverly describing Catherine (as his sister realizes), and thus obliquely indicating his own appreciation of her.

Chapter 26

The Tilneys believe that Isabella's lack of fortune will count adversely with the General should any marriage with Captain Tilney be contemplated, but they feel that Frederick is not serious and is unlikely to come to Northanger Abbey. Henry must go to Woodston, and the General suggests that they all visit him there. Catherine has to wait until Wednesday for the visit, but she delights in the place, and the General 's comments give a strong impression that he envisages marriage between Catherine and Henry. But Catherine, delightful though the day has been, still does not know what Henry's feelings are.

Commentary

Catherine has the independence not to be convinced by Henry and Eleanor that the General is merely mercenary, though in fact her own self-interest is guiding her judgement, since she is in love with Henry and is sensitive about her own 'portionless' state. That love is emphasized in her contemplation of Woodston despite the grandiose accompaniment to her thoughts by the General. Indeed he is so overbearing that Catherine's own praises are inhibited. Nevertheless it is apparent that the General has designed her for Henry (that is, presuming she is an heiress). There is something repugnant about the gourmet fastidiousness of General Tilney.

canvassed Discussed.
portionless Without a dowry, i.e. wealth to bring to a husband.
half a buck Venison, deer.
ready-monied . . . happiness . . . draft on the future i.e. what we find happy now may only be a loan, and the future may not be happy. The image is odd coming from Henry, but perhaps he is aware of the store set by his father on money and position. He cannot be aware of Catherine's future suffering, though this present happiness is almost outweighed by the ungenerous treatment she is to receive in the future.
Newfoundland puppy Very large, shaggy water-dog from the island of that name in North America.
a bow thrown out i.e. a bow window.
a patched on bow i.e. a window added.

Chapter 27

This brief chapter contains the letter from Isabella; it is described as a 'strain of shallow artifice'. She acknowledges Catherine's two letters, and says that she is quite uneasy about James, who has gone to Oxford. She elaborates by saying that the man she most dislikes, Captain Tilney, has left, having carried on with other girls, and urges Catherine to write to James on her behalf. This of course Catherine will not do, and she confides in her friends, who endorse her opinion of Isabella as a 'vain coquette', but say that Frederick has too strong a head to injure himself romantically.

Commentary

Jane Austen is here employing the epistolary style of Richardson to further the narration and plot. The insight into the character of Isabella is definite – she is shallow, has obviously been dropped by Captain Tilney, is seeking to win her way back into Catherine's good graces, and is completely superficial, hypocritical, ill-bred and undiscriminating in everything that she does and says. Catherine reacts strongly – it is again a mark of her growing independence and increased maturity of judgement as a result of being in the company of Eleanor and Henry.

coxcomg Conceited show-off, showy man.
your mind is warped by . . . general integrity This is very fine compliment from Henry, showing how much, by putting things in this inverted way, he appreciates Catherine's complete integrity and sincerity.

Chapter 28

The General goes away to London for a week, and Catherine is aware of a new atmosphere of ease. Henry is away at Woodston and one afternoon the two girls hear a prolonged ringing of the house-bell. Eleanor goes, and when she returns Catherine is told that she must leave Northanger early the next morning on the instructions of the General. Eleanor is upset, so is Catherine, and both wonder whatever she has done to offend the General that he should behave in this uncompromising way. Catherine spends a terrible night – as the result of real worry, unlike that first one, which was out of imagination and simulated fear – and then at six in the morning Eleanor comes to her. She begs Catherine to write to her, gives her money for her journey home, sensing that she needs it, and embraces her. Catherine is too moved even to mention Henry's name.

Commentary

There is a charming exchange between Eleanor and Catherine on the subject of Catherine's going away. Eleanor is kind, Henry – obviously in love with Catherine though this is unknown to her – gratified. The surprise arrival of the carriage makes for dramatic tension, and this is followed by the behaviour of Eleanor, conscious that she has been forced into this unwelcome errand to Catherine. We note the spontaneity of Catherine's response – generous in order to spare her friend worry – and revealing of Eleanor's capacity for feeling at the same time because of her father's inexcusable and ill-bred behaviour in getting rid of Catherine so quickly and without courtesy. Catherine is of course humiliated, but the interaction between the two girls, with Eleanor's generosity in providing her with money, provides an emotional and moving sequence.

post i.e. post-chaise, public as distinct from private conveyance.
repast Meal.
Alice The maid, so that no one would suspect who had written.

Chapter 29

Largely a description of Catherine's overwrought feelings during the early part of the journey, particularly as she passes the turning which would have led her to Woodston. The author uses her own voice to describe satirically the degraded manner in which her heroine (as distinct from those of more fashionable romances) returns to her home in the hack post-chaise. Despite this, Catherine receives a joyful welcome from her family; she tells them what has happened and, although her parents are offended for her sake, they take a more balanced and obviously less subjective view of the case. Catherine writes briefly to Eleanor, enclosing the money which she owes her. She then calls on the Allens, and finds Mr Allen critical of the General's conduct – Mrs Allen repeating her husband's views without for one moment understanding their implication. At this stage Mrs Morland proves that she does not understand what is going on in her daughter's mind.

Commentary

Catherine at every turn of the early part of the journey reveals her unvoiced love for Henry. So sensitive is Catherine that she believes it possible that the General is offended because of what she dared to think about him. The revelations of Catherine's consciousness give way to the omniscient comment on the manner of her heroine's return, a nicely balanced parody of the romantic-heroic set against the somewhat sordid reality. Although Catherine has not wished to reach the end of her journey, the welcome, the family greetings and atmosphere, are a testimony to real feelings as distinct from the simulated ones which Catherine has had a full share of from Isabella and General Tilney. Mrs Morland only half understands Catherine's feelings for Henry, but she shows herself to be of sound common sense in suggesting the visit to Mrs Allen. Mrs Allen proves to be as vacuous as ever.

postmasters i.e. those in charge of the post-chaises.
But my affair is widely different Note that the author has let her heroine's affairs proceed through her own consciousness, and has not therefore

interrupted the narrative flow. But now the author is herself conscious – in a mock-pompous way of her responsibilities as a novelist, and accordingly sets this returning scene – reality – as a contrast to what happens so often in romance.

shatter-brained Presumably a variant of 'scatter-brained'.
amendment i.e. improvement in behaviour (and situation).
Mechlin A type of lace from Belgium.

Chapter 30

Catherine's loss of spirits and her inability to apply herself to work for any length of time are described. Her mother naturally accuses her of fretting, but Catherine is overjoyed when Henry Tilney arrives unexpectedly. On the excuse of paying his respects to Mr and Mrs Allen, he walks with Catherine towards their house and proposes to her. His father has ordered him to forget her, so he is, in fact, proposing against the General's wishes.

It now turns out that the General was misled by John Thorpe into thinking that Catherine was of great social status and fortune. He then discovered from the same source (Thorpe's own disappointment over Catherine had infuriated him) – that the family are very poor. This in its turn is an exaggeration, but the General accepts it; Henry expresses deep shame on his father's account, but it does not alter his love for Catherine.

Commentary

Catherine is both restless and depressed, though the actual nature of this is rather misinterpreted by Mrs Morland, perhaps an indication of the real gap between mother and daughter. Catherine is, ironically in view of her individuality, behaving rather like a romantic heroine in a decline for her lost love. That lost love is fortunately found – and Mrs Morland shows herself equal to the occasion in understanding, sympathy and warmth. Henry shows his own grasp of the situation by contriving to get Catherine alone, and asserts not only his love for Catherine but his independence of his father's wishes by proposing to her. Yet an authorial comment suggests that he has grown to love her because he is sure that she loves him. Catherine is human enough to experience a 'triumphant delight' when she learns the details of the General's behaviour. The plot strands are now tied up. Thorpe had misled the General, and the latter's violence, always latent, has now been released against any connection with Catherine. It says much for Henry's stability and constancy that he is able to make his own decision with regard to Catherine. The author frankly spells out all the details. We are left with a feeling of contempt for the General, and rejoice in Catherine's unconscious triumph.

time for balls and plays, and a time for work Perhaps Mrs Morland is herself aware of the Biblical echo here.

The Mirror See Pan note, p.236.

a persuasion of her partiality for him The idea that she was in love with him (had in turn originally caused his own response to her).

It is a new circumstance in romance Here the author is asserting equality in love, which is dependent on feeling and will, and it is not the prerogative of the male sex to be first to express it.

vouchers i.e. guarantees.

rhodomontade Boastful bragging.

Chapter 31

Mr Tilney asks Mr and Mrs Morland if he may marry Catherine. All they stipulate is the consent of the General; when Eleanor Tilney makes an extremely desirable marriage, she prevails upon the General to change his mind. He does so with great condescension – aided by the fact that he finds Thorpe has exaggerated the real state and status of the Morlands! The novel ends with a superbly ironic remark of the author's: 'I leave it to be settled by whomsoever it may concern, whether the tendency of this work be altogether to recommend parental tyranny, or reward filial disobedience.'

Commentary

The omniscient author bulks largely in this final chapter, and we may feel that the marriage of Eleanor Tilney is a convenient plot device to bring about the happiness of Henry and Catherine. Eleanor's becoming 'Your Ladyship' is compensation for the General, though we must feel, with the author, that he doesn't deserve it. That this is the way of the world is Jane Austen's unvoiced but accurate moral comment. The fact that Catherine is to have three thousand pounds of her own is a further comment on the inaccuracy of John Thorpe and the impetuosity of General Tilney. The ironic remark quoted above reflects the necessary ambivalence of the author who has tried to present things as they are in life, rather than as they are represented in romantic fiction.

Revision questions on Chapters 21–31

1 How does Jane Austen achieve tension and comedy in her account of Catherine's first night at the Abbey?

2 Describe the roles played by Henry and Eleanor in Catherine's stay at the Abbey.

3 What does Catherine learn about herself and about life from her period at Northanger?

4 Write an account of her parents' reception of Catherine on her return home in disgrace, and their reaction to Henry's proposal to her.

5 In your opinion, is the novel ended in a satisfactory way? Give reasons for your answer.

Jane Austen's art in *Northanger Abbey*
The characters

Catherine Morland

> But when a young lady is to be a heroine, the perverseness of forty surrounding families cannot prevent her. Something must and will happen to throw a hero in her way.

The opening chapter of the novel traces Catherine's early life, first as a plain, sallow-faced tomboy, through the years to the inexperienced and impressionable, but reasonably pretty, seventeen-year-old who sets off for Bath with the Allens. Once Jane Austen conducts her heroine into the world of sophistication and experience epitomized by those she meets in Bath, she develops as a character. Catherine is, despite her author's satire, a *real* heroine, for her responses are those of an honest, forthright, self-conscious but totally disarming girl. The world, in the shape of Isabella Thorpe, John Thorpe and General Tilney, and even the dress-oriented Mrs Allen, can take advantage of her, but her essential integrity is never undermined, and she responds from the human heart in ignorance of the conventions of the fashionable head.

Catherine running to tell the Tilneys that John Thorpe had no right to beg her off her commitment to them; Catherine anxiously telling Henry at the theatre how sorry she was that she had already gone out when they called, is recognizably kin to that Elizabeth Bennet of *Pride and Prejudice* who walks through the wet grass to see how her sick sister Jane is progressing at Netherfield, thus disgusting the Bingley sisters by her impetuous (and warm) flouting of convention. Catherine and Elizabeth are both of their limited class and time, yet both of them transcend the limitations. Catherine is normal enough to feel bored (and later yawns) when she has attended her first ball and no one has noticed her until she is leaving. She is impressionable enough to be completely taken in by Isabella's attentions and professions of undying friendship, but proud enough to be indignant at the blatant contradictions and inconsistencies of John Thorpe (particularly when he represents her brother James to be a drinking man). She is naive and artless enough to let the rather sophisticated Henry Tilney know where her heart lies, and susceptible enough to feel the power of Mrs Radcliffe's novels on the one hand and that factual corollary to Mrs Radcliffe, the Abbey, on the other. Most of the novel is experienced through Catherine's consciousness – her simple longing to see Henry who has been so polite and considerate to her, her unawareness that in his gross and insensitive way John Thorpe is actually proposing to her – and finally her gradual coming to see into and through her 'friend' Isabella's fickle and facile behaviour.

Catherine always embodies the moral standards that are at the core of the novel; subject to the vicissitudes of location, whether in Bath or at the Abbey, she remains constant in her inherent and inherited decency. Isabella cannot move these standards, nor can the General diminish them. When Catherine cries it is because she is young, innocent and vulnerable, but she has also a genuine sensitivity, which knows that in thinking the General may have been responsible for his wife's death she has been guilty of inconsiderate and wrong-minded thoughts – that the sensational novels she devours in no way approximate to the moral criteria by which people live. If Catherine is deficient in anything it is perhaps in a developed sense of humour, though one hopes that under Henry's tutelage this will come.

Northanger Abbey is largely about the education of Catherine's feelings, for gradually she comes to see that Eleanor Tilney, and of course Henry, represent culture, taste and moral rectitude – as distinct from the superficial, flighty and wholly selfish actions of creatures like Isabella. Catherine is timid but not negative; she speaks her mind whatever costs she must suffer by so doing. She is impetuous but is capable of changing her mind, as when she decides that she will write to Eleanor despite the fact that the moral castigation of the General means that he would not allow his daughter to receive letters from her. She is ingenuous and romantic, looking to see Henry in the theatre or at one of the other centres in Bath, but the determined coquetry that informs Isabella's actions, and indeed her reflexes, is entirely absent from Catherine. She is loath to think ill of anybody, though she is seriously disturbed by Isabella's flirting with Captain Tilney, comforting herself that the last night she spent in Bath with James and Isabella shows the pair to be apparently contented with each other.

Catherine is at all times apprehensive of the General; if the word were not too strong it would be true to say that she dislikes him. But the centre of Catherine's life is Henry Tilney after that first interesting meeting and conversation; balancing this is her fascination with the sensational fiction she reads and therefore her strange appraisal of the Abbey and its terror-and-mystery potential. All this is of course part of the education of her character and feelings to which we have referred; she sees fear in every closet, mysteries in chests, corridors and apartments – with the dead Mrs Tilney's room the focus of it all. All these, together with such exciting speculation at the General's papers perused after midnight – and the washing-bill awaiting the light of day (and reason) – are the small crises that stimulate the delicious flutter of fear.

Nevertheless, Catherine invariably behaves well, without affectation or self-interest, and the only time she exhibits true romantic melancholia is when, arrived back at her home in Fullerton, she cannot set her mind to any useful work – due not only to her feelings of having been unjustly treated, but above all because she is miserable at the thought that she may not see Henry again. All *is* well that ends well, but practically and imaginatively Catherine has come a long way from Fullerton. She has seen the fashionable world, and survived it by her own good sense and integrity, rejecting affectation and maintaining her own honesty and truth despite the various temptations. Catherine always acts on principle, and loyalty to her friends and to an exacting code of conduct are her priorities whatever she is called upon to do or say. Consequently we never feel that Catherine is merely silly, for her impressionability is always tinctured with sincerity and the genuineness of response.

As the narrative proceeds, so Jane Austen's irony leaves her heroine – in much the same way as George Eliot's leaves Dorothea Brooke in *Middlemarch* – and Catherine stands in her own right as a likeable, insecure, apprehensive but forthright and considerate girl who is aware of her own shortcomings and charmingly transcends them by the disarming naturalness of her character and her manner.

Henry Tilney

He seemed to be about four or five and twenty, was rather tall, had a pleasing countenance, a very intelligent and lively eye, and, if not quite handsome, was very near it. His address was good . . .

No satirical commentary accompanies the introduction of Henry Tilney to the reader, and he obviously has never needed to go into training to be a hero. He is none the less satirical himself, and we note how delightfully he sends up the fops and society climbers of Bath in his first conversation with Catherine. But he is courteous, considerate, kind, obviously silently aware of Catherine's inexperience, and delicately determined not to wound her in any way beyond the natural one of joking at the expense of society, and gently in compliment to her. He is not frivolous, he is not irresponsible, he is not a rattle and, best of all, he is not a bore, but a cultivated, intelligent, charming and well-informed man. He is seen to good advantage whenever he appears, but particularly in Bath, for James Morland is dull, John Thorpe is objectionable and Mr Allen prefers the quietude of the card-room to his wife's inconsequential dress-centred chatter.

Henry has discrimination and taste, and Catherine is influenced by both, particularly in the walk up Beechen Hill, with the delightful and effortless discussion about sketching and perspective that occupies brother and sister. Henry presents, too, a direct contrast with his brother, for he is not a flirt and neither ego-centric nor heartless. He is in good contrast to his father too, for he is not conscious of status or money, his own fine character protecting him from the lures of the materialistic world. Woodston, not the Abbey, is his haven, his retreat and his life – modest but tasteful, rich in the simple attributes of existence and the fulfilment to be obtained from these. There are no exaggerations in Henry apart from his delightful sense of the satirical (though he, too, we notice was fascinated by *The Mysteries of Udolpho* despite his initial cynicism.)

Henry's severity is always tempered by justice, so that when Catherine apologizes to him at the theatre he softens because of her obvious agitation. When he disturbs Catherine in his mother's apartment at the Abbey, he sees fit, in a kind of salutary indulgence, to give her a somewhat detailed account of his mother's death and the expert medical attendance she had. But again his severity is tempered here by another kind of justice which, since the novel is about sensationalism and reality, is essential to Catherine's development. He feels, just as we do, that Catherine has let herself down harbouring wholly horror-associated thoughts about the General and his doings. This really indicates his concern for Catherine, not that she shall be worthy of him but worthy of the true and pure individual he knows her to be. Perhaps this is the first indication too of his love for her.

His conversation is a perpetual delight – full of good sense, wit and taste; he has the ease of the gentleman without any of the affectation that sometimes accompanies a consciousness of naturally inherited or achieved worldly status. He adapts with ease to any situation, treating Mrs Allen's remarks on Catherine's gown with becoming gravity (though there may be much inward laughter): 'I do not think it will wash well; I am afraid it will fray.' He saves the best of his satire for Catherine's account of the next and most terrible horror novel to be published, capping his remarks with a superb imaginative fiction of his own, the sheer exuberance of which demonstrates one of Henry's most attractive features. His other most endearing action is his following Catherine to Fullerton after she has been unceremoniously turned away from the Abbey; without being overtly critical of his father, he is certainly aware of the different codes and expectations by which they live. And when he has proposed to Catherine, and confessed the true nature of his feelings, we are pleased to note that he 'talked at random, without sense or connection', a sure indication that Henry has succumbed to love and is temporarily without that control and measure of utterance we have come to expect from him.

This is the last significant humanizing touch in the author's presentation of his character – and how much we appreciate the fact that Catherine gets the man she deserves, and whose momentary tremulousness and emotionalism show that he has a sensibility so fittingly corresponding to hers. If we had had any criticism of Henry it might have been that he lacked emotional fullness, but this reassurance adds greater completeness to his character.

Isabella Thorpe

the graceful spirit of her walk, the fashionable air of her figure and dress . . . 'The men think us incapable of real friendship you know, and I am determined to show them the difference.'

Isabella just escapes being caricature, but despite her beauty there is something grotesque about her. It consists largely of her conversation, which is a running commentary on a flighty, insincere, self-centred and wholly worthless character. There does not seem to be one redeeming feature in her make-up. Her behaviour and her attitudes are characterized by inconsistency: witness her description of the two odious young men, then her subterfuge of setting out with Catherine to follow them; her saying she will not dance, that she will never leave Catherine's side, then of course dancing; her affair with Captain Tilney, which she never acknowledges; and basically her expressions of friendship for Catherine which turn out to be a hollow sham. Lastly, there is the letter she writes to Catherine, largely one of injured innocence, in which she asks Catherine to intercede with James on her behalf by writing to him – yet further evidence perhaps of her self-deception as well as an attempt to mislead others.

Her chatter is as inconsequential as Mrs Allen's: she is incapable of concentration or of keeping to one topic. She must have her will – witness the drives to Blaize Castle and to Clifton – and she is ill-mannered, ill-bred, inconsiderate, gratifying her own whims and indulging her own pleasures – though it might be argued that she is never still enough to have any. In a word she is silly; she is also frivolous and sensation-seeking, though one suspects that she only reads the salacious or terrifying episodes in the novels she mentions as conversation fodder, later to be retailed to someone as ingenuous as Catherine. She is jealous – witness Miss Andrews – and possessive over James, though she hardly pays him any attention. In her own family she rules the roost – her sisters imitate her, and one of them accompanies her on a drive as a privilege when Catherine is firm enough to put the Tilneys first and refuse to go on the drive.

Isabella is an inveterate gossip, an unprincipled coquette, lacks a sense of humour, plays cards (it has been suggested that this is part of her matrimonial gambles or perhaps symbolizes them), has no taste, is constantly distracted, feigns emotions at the drop of a fan, and considers that her brother is a model of behaviour. In short, Isabella has no real substance; beneath the chat there is nothing that we can call character, beneath the superficial attraction nothing that we can call personality, beneath the affectations and protestations nothing that we can call truth. She is the antithesis of the heroine, particularly the Gothic heroine. In a sense, she deserves Captain Tilney but lacks, of course, any knowledge of his resistant heart; in short, he makes a fool of her, and we may say of Isabella that she is all fizz and no sparkle.

Eleanor Tilney

Miss Tilney met her with great civility, returned her advances with equal good will, and they continued talking together as long as both parties remained in the room . . .

Eleanor Tilney is the obvious contrast to Isabella, though she has not so great a part in the narrative as that female rattle. She is quiet, reserved, well-bred, considerate, correctly chaperoned by Mrs Hughes, obviously dotes on her brother Henry, and equally obviously is well under the paternal thumb of the General, who exacts obedience from his children almost as the reflex of his own being. Consequently Eleanor does not emerge as a character in her own right until Catherine's visit to the Abbey. She understands Catherine and treats her with great courtesy informed by warmth, and this may well be because she suspects that beneath Henry's thinking and reserved exterior he is really interested in Catherine and may well be falling in love with her. Like her brother, she has discerning taste, and seeks out the quietly beautiful areas of Bath with more enthusiasm than she does the fashionable ones.

Isabella, of course, proclaims that Eleanor is beautiful, but there is an inner beauty about her that we might perhaps more correctly call sincerity. Eleanor is *good* without being cloying: her enjoyments are sketching, painting, walking; she has a natural reserve of both expression and manner. When with Henry, she tends to be somewhat overshadowed, with the General she is at the mercy of his moods; despite this, her good breeding and her concern for others stand her in good stead. In a sense she is unworldly, for when Catherine speaks of the forthcoming major event in London, it is Henry who has to enlighten his sister that Catherine is merely talking about a novel. Eleanor is a great defender of history as against fiction, but she is always gracious and kind, and Catherine is in the forefront of her consideration.

Isabella has accused her of pride (of course without knowing her), but Eleanor is not proud, merely reserved and obedient in her own father's home. We are told that 'she took pains' to be near Catherine, and we suspect that she too is worried by her elder brother's irresponsible behaviour, for the Captain may have something in common with his father, since he has little to do with his brother and sister. Eleanor is a little embarrassed about inviting Catherine to the Abbey (after all, she has been put up to it by her father), but we are told that she 'was earnest, though gentle, in her secondary civilities', and indeed the word 'gentle' seems to be a good summary of Eleanor's salient feature. But at the Abbey she becomes Catherine's real friend as distinct from the artificial relationship Catherine has had with Isabella.

Throughout Henry's Gothic banter Eleanor remains serious, aware always of her responsibilities to her guest – they must not be late for meals for fear of offending the General: indeed keeping the domestic peace is one of Eleanor's main concerns. There is a certain melancholy in her nature too, and Catherine becomes her confidante regarding her late mother; it obviously distressed Eleanor at the time – and has continued to distress her through the years – that she was away from home when her mother was taken ill and died. In a sense, though perhaps not a serious one, she has the wish for seclusion and retirement which charactrizes some of the heroines of Gothic romance, but there is certainly no irony in the tone that describes this harmless indulgence of Eleanor's: 'I have no sister you know – and though Henry – though my brothers are very affectionate, and Henry is a great deal here, which I am most thankful for, it is impossible for me not to be often solitary.' What a wealth of concealment and admission there is here – the determination to be as loyal to Frederick as to Henry, and yet admitting the loneliness that drives her back in upon herself.

Eleanor's melancholy, and the fact that she was away when her mother died, unfortunately add fuel to Catherine's Gothic flame, and she suspects the worst about the death. But Eleanor's sterling qualities are apparent when, after her father has ordered her to dismiss Catherine summarily from the premises, she does her utmost to ameliorate the sufferings and the insult that Catherine now has to endure. We suspect that she is aware of her brother's inclinations too, for the visit to Woodston had seen Eleanor, in the nicest possible way (compare the General), viewing Catherine as her future sister-in-law. In asking her to write, Eleanor puts friendship above family obedience, and we respect her for it. There is something delightfully ironic in the fact that it is she who achieves what the General covets – status. The thought of the General calling her 'my Ladyship', and the knowledge that she effects the reconciliation between father and son, make Eleanor an attractive if somewhat under-written character.

John Thorpe

> He was a stout young man of middling height, who with a plain face and ungraceful form, seemed fearful of being too handsome unless he wore the dress of a groom, and too much like a gentleman unless he were easy where he ought to be civil, and impudent where he might be allowed to be easy.

One is tempted to say that John Thorpe is every inch Isabella's brother, and that in presenting them Jane Austen has given them a family psychology that is sharply and convincingly delineated. He has his sister's loquacity but without any of the superficial sophistication that attends her; he is ill-bred to even the most obvious observer. His passion is his horse and gig, and he is intent upon showing them off (though he has obviously made a bad bargain). He exaggerates everything, so that any journey he undertakes is distorted in terms of length and the time taken to do it. He is a braggart; never listens to what anyone else has to say; patronizes his friend Morland (who is misguided enough to think only good of him); has no social manners; condescends to his mother and younger sisters. One cannot see him at any time as an Oxford man, though there is reason to think that his type was not uncommon during the early part of the nineteenth century.

In addition to the limitations indicated above, Thorpe ingratiates himself with General Tilney by exaggerating Catherine's position and inheritance and that of the Allens; and then, when his own and Isabella's disappointments are at full tide, reverses the story so completely that the Morland family are represented as impoverished. This shows just how unscrupulous he is, and though, earlier on, Isabella can assure Catherine that John is in love with her, his proposal – clumsy, indelicate, as devious as he is himself – is a piece of pure opportunism. Just as his sister is something of a gold-digger (witness her ill-concealed disappointment at the amount of Mr Morland's proposed provision for herself and James) so John Thorpe is the social climber whose arrogance and bombast, he imagines, will see him to success.

There is nothing more insensitive in the novel than his going to Miss Tilney to excuse Catherine from an appointment with the Tilneys, when she manifestly does not wish to be excused; driving her a long distance against her will; imposing on her by proposing obliquely because he thinks it will be to his advantage. Hypocrite is too strong a word for Thorpe; he is a dangerous 'rattle', dangerous because he thinks only of himself, has no moral standards, and is quite capable of injuring others by his thoughtlessness and arrogance. He is materialistic, unpredictable, lacking in judgement, honesty, truthfulness or even an iota of moral fibre.

General Tilney

He was a very handsome man, of a commanding aspect, past the bloom, but not past the vigour of life; and with his eye still directed towards her, she saw him presently address Mr Tilney in a familiar whisper.

If John Thorpe is the ill-bred, undiscriminating opportunist, General Tilney is the larger-than-life autocrat with an eye permanently on the main social chance. We are told that his epitaph to his wife is 'highly-strained' and that it reflected the 'inconsolable husband', and we guess that she was part of the Abbey, part of the fittings of a life consciously bent towards material advancement and acquisition from pineries to Gothic pillars. The General rules; his children rigidly observe the meaningless ritual of an arid punctuality. His pride is the pride of possessions and status; he is a man of moods and of a certain irascibility; he is impatient, abrupt, acts precipitously, and reprimands (perhaps a reflex of his rank and duties) fall readily from his lips. In a good mood he has a kind of old-world courtesy; he is self-important, aware of his rank in society and indeed in the country at large, for he reads his newspaper as if it were an important dispatch, and sits up at night to study papers which supposedly have a national importance.

The General sets great store by show, by what appears rather than what is. It gives him great pleasure to know that in bulk and produce and modernity his gardens and hot-houses are far in advance of Mr Allen's. But he is not a man of true dignity of position; he is inquisitive and complacent, acquisitive and snobbish, unworthy to be the father of Henry and Eleanor, and perhaps having more in common with Captain Tilney, also with the social climbers who are far beneath him. It says little for his intelligence and discrimination that he should believe what a rattle like John Thorpe says to him, and it says less for his humanity that he should subject a 17-year-old guest to a long, unaccompanied journey because she does not possess the fortune he thought she had. Fundamentally the General appears to lack the breeding (except ostentatiously on occasions) that his two good children unquestionably possess; he is a spoilt, worldly and unpleasant man.

Mrs Allen

Dress was her passion. She had a most harmless delight in being fine . . .

Mrs Allen is essential to the plot, since it is her function – Mr Allen generally being otherwise sensibly engaged – to take Catherine into Society, though she herself knows nobody in Bath prior to that fortuitous meeting with Mrs Thorpe. Mrs Allen is seen ironically throughout, but with a degree of tolerance and kindliness despite her excessive stupidity and sense of show. She is complacent in her social attitudes, but she gets several fillips from her meetings with Mrs Thorpe: a sense of her own superiority in dress and status; the knowledge that she now has someone to talk to without listening much in return (Mrs Thorpe effortlessly adopts the same practice since she does not require an articulate audience.) She sometimes listens to Mr Allen, the sublime example of this occurring near the end of the novel where she repeats with diminishing understanding Mr Allen's evaluation of the General's conduct.

Mrs Allen's one fear is that she will injure her dress, while the staple diet of her conversation is an unrelieved commentary on the price of dress materials and the durability and attractiveness of her own or other people's apparel. She is a silly woman, but harmless, and she and Mr Allen represent almost a foretaste, in a less significant form, of the satirical appraisal of marriage seen in Mr and Mrs Bennet in *Pride and Prejudice* – the Allens are a preliminary study in non-communication in marriage.

Mr Allen

The author gives the sensible, self-effacing Mr Allen much less space than his wife. He suffers from gout, hence the need for his visit to Bath for the waters; he prefers the card-room to the ball-room, returning when all is over to escort the ladies home. He has Catherine's well-being at heart, however, for he takes pains to find out if Henry Tilney is a suitable acquaintance for her. He appears but sparsely in the action of the narrative, but when Catherine returns to Fullerton, ignominiously expelled by the General from the Abbey, we are told that Mr Allen 'expressed himself on the occasion with the reasonable resentment of a sensible friend'. He is moderate and balanced, kind and interested in Catherine and, as far as we can see, less Society-conscious than those we meet in Bath.

Mrs Thorpe

Mrs Thorpe is a widow, and nicely balances Mrs Allen in the action of Chapter 4; the author indulges in delightful irony at their expense:

> Their joy on this meeting was very great, as well it might, since they had been contented to know nothing of each other for the last fifteen years (p. 36).

Mrs Thorpe's advantage, if such it can be called, is that although she is a widow, she has a family of children to talk about, and this she does at great length. Mrs Allen has to be content with the fact that 'the lace on Mrs Thorpe's pelisse was not half so handsome as that on her own'. We are told that Mrs Thorpe is good-humoured and well-meaning, but the fact that she is a 'very indulgent mother' means that John and Isabella are thought perfect where the reverse is the case. The younger Thorpe girls are completely in the shadow of their obnoxious elder siblings, but manage to convey at least that they are of the same ilk in terms of unpleasantness: 'Maria's intelligence concluded with a tender effusion of pity for her sister Anne, whom she represented as insupportably cross, from being excluded the party.'

Mrs Morland

Mrs Morland strikes one as a woman of sound common sense, for Catherine has been brought up by her mother and father on positive, though not repressive, moral principles; on her return home it is her mother who notices the signs of her unhappiness and who counsels her to concentrate on her work. Catherine's account of her treatment at the hands of the General leads to rather moderate offence on her account from her essentially down-to-earth parents, for although Mrs Morland is described as 'philosophical' she also has a practical turn which causes her to ask Catherine whether she has left anything behind in any of her pockets! But she is philosophic about Catherine meeting Henry 'in the course of a few years', though she takes some pride in the fact that by making her own way home Catherine has proved that she can 'shift very well for herself'. The whole course of Mrs Morland's feelings in the matter is changed by the arrival of Henry, whom she receives 'with the simple professions of unaffected benevolence'. She has her husband withhold their consent to Catherine's marriage until the General gives his; let it be said, however, that this 'very courteously worded in a page full of empty professions to Mr Morland' indicates the ingrained condescension of the General.

James Morland

Catherine's brother is a disappointment. Although from time to time he dilutes the exaggerations of John Thorpe, he does not see through the falseness of Isabella until it is much too late, and his letter to Catherine is weak – an indication that his errors of judgement are not likely to end with Isabella. It is one thing to be trusting, another to be blind or to excuse what is inexcusable.

Captain Tilney

A passing caricature, a brief pencil-sketch of other Jane Austen heart-triflers to come, like Wickham and Henry Crawford. He hasn't a heart himself, and one feels that Isabella merits his cavalier treatment if only because of her own vapid and mindless flirtations.

All the characters in the book are vivified by the quality of their dialogue.

Style and narrative art

As Mary Lascelles has said, 'Jane Austen had found that she was able to return, cool and critical, to work that she had laid by, and to better it.' This certainly appears to be the approach to *Northanger Abbey*, earlier called *Susan*, though there were moments of pessimism which caused her to observe that 'Miss Catherine is put upon the shelf for the present . . . and I do not know that she will ever come out.' Miss Lascelles believes that Jane Austen had been reading Barrett's burlesque novel *The Heroine* in 1814, and that this may have precipitated her return to the manuscript of *Northanger Abbey* since it 'must have shown her that the time for mocking false romance was not yet past'. Her brother had re-purchased the copyright for her, so that we have before us, in a peculiar sense, an early and a later work of Jane Austen's, and the stylistic gain is a great one.

Jane Austen is one of the most complete and accomplished stylists writing in our language; every word is weighed, and yet there is a sense of almost effortless fluency. Her descriptions are straightforward and harmonious, providing us with clear pictures, whether they be of movements or scenes. Her dialogue is natural and unforced, a verbal index to the character and personality of each speaker. Her wit is various but always expressed with taste and insight, while her irony and, in this novel, her satire, are flames that kindle the objects of her censure. Pope, whom she greatly admired, and who died some fifty or more years before she began to write, has said in a typical couplet much that summarizes Jane Austen's achievement and the dedication necessary to bring it about:

True ease in writing comes from art, not chance
As those move easiest who have learnt to dance.

And we know from the numerous revisions to the manuscripts that Jane was a meticulous and painstaking craftswoman. The early burlesques have in *Northanger Abbey* a later equivalent, for here is a careful parody of the Gothic mood in atmosphere and innuendo, particularly in the Abbey scenes. But the influence of the Augustan age, of Pope, of the somewhat austere and balanced expression of poets like Gray, Cowper, Thomson, the superb rhetorical prose and converse of Dr Johnson, together with the latter's awareness of the conservative and historical force of language, all influenced her style.

Jane Austen learned much, too, from the didactic morality of Richardson in his epistolary style and perhaps also appreciated the elegance and society dialogue of Fanny Burney in *Camilla* and *Cecilia*. But Jane's own elegance, directness and singular rightness of emphasis, her taste and form, are not derivative. Her writing is the product of a logical, disciplined, well-read and refined intellect working on the basic material of human nature: its domestic life; its social intercourse; its falling in and out of love; its pretensions and pride; its breeding and true humility.

First, we might note the opening of the novel, which immediately strikes the ironic note so characteristic of Jane Austen: 'No one who had ever seen Catherine Morland in her infancy, would have supposed her born to be an heroine' (p.21). Heroines are found in fiction and in plays, and one of the major aspects of Jane Austen's style in *Northanger Abbey* is her burlesquing of her fellow writers and their particular obsessions. One of these would be the perfection and beauty of their heroines; from the outset Jane makes it clear that Catherine is more ordinary than outstanding. All the traditional usages are therefore reversed in her treatment of Catherine: her mother does not die in childbirth; Catherine herself is a tomboy for much of her young life; she is far from accomplished, being only too glad when the music-master leaves. The *ironic* mode – and the whole of the first chapter is written in this vein, even to the private joke about Mr Morland's name being Richard, has many variants as the novel progresses. Thus Mrs Allen is seen ironically; here she is in the full serenity of dress-preservation:

> Mrs Allen congratulated herself, as soon as they were seated, on having preserved her gown from injury. 'It would have been very shocking to have it torn,' said she, 'would it not? – It is such a delicate muslin. – For my part I have not seen any thing I like so well in the whole room, I assure you' (Chap. 2, p.29).

Here is a lightness of touch which is, in a sense, misleading, for the morality inherent in Jane Austen's style is clear – this is an example of selfishness, and the lightness with which it is treated indicates that the culpability is not too great. When she comes to treat the General, almost at the very end of the novel, irony and plain statement cohere in strong moral combination to underline the author's stance:

... and that Catherine would have three thousand pounds. This was so material an amendment of his late expectations, that it greatly contributed to smooth the descent of his pride; and by no means without its effect was the private intelligence, which he was at some pains to procure, that the Fullerton estate, being entirely at the disposal of its present proprietor, was consequently open to every greedy speculation.

On the strength of this, the General, soon after Eleanor's marriage, permitted his son to return to Northanger, and thence made him the bearer of his consent, very courteously worded in a page full of empty professions to Mr Morland (Chap. 31, p.229).

The key words are 'greedy' and 'empty'; we now see Mrs Allen's selfishness in perspective, and both ironically and morally, castigate the General for what he is and for what he represents. It is difficult to avoid the conclusion that Jane Austen's irony is her way of moralizing, but without any of the sententiousness sometimes attached to a pronouncement. She does not pronounce, she indicates; and where she is not direct she is wittily oblique, though she leaves the reader in no doubt as to the rights and wrongs, the propriety or otherwise, of what her characters do in particular situations.

The quality of Jane Austen's irony is not always gentle: Isabella Thorpe is a salient case in point. Consider the ironic exposure of hypocrisy in Isabella's letter to Catherine.

You know I have a pretty good spirit of my own. Anne Mitchell had tried to put on a turban like mine, as I wore it the week before at the Concert, but made wretched work of it – it happened to become my odd face I believe, at least Tilney told me so at the time, and said every eye was upon me; but he is the last man whose word I would take. I wear nothing but purple now: I know I look hideous in it, but no matter – it is your dear brother's favourite colour (Chap. 27, p.199).

Again the author's moral censure is evident: vanity, insincerity, inconsistency and irresponsibility, with Isabella in purple a kind of equivalent to the cross-gartered Malvolio of *Twelfth Night.* All this is of the essence of sardonic irony; the lightness of touch has gone.

At other times the irony exists solely in the nature of the dialogue; here is Catherine with the Allens, each unaware of the thoughts of the others until speech clarifies error and re-establishes taste or, in the case of Mrs Allen, meaningless repetition:

'No; I had just engaged myself to walk with Miss Tilney before they told me of it; and therefore you know I could not go with them, could I?'

'No, certainly not; and I am glad you did not think of it. These schemes are not at all the thing. Young men and women driving about the country in open carriages! Now and then it is very well; but going to inns and public places together! It is not right; and I wonder Mrs Thorpe should allow it. I am glad you do not think of going; I am sure Mrs Morland would not be pleased. Mrs Allen, are not you of my way of thinking? Do not you think these kind of projects objectionable?'

'Yes, very much so indeed. Open carriages are nasty things. A clean gown is not five minutes' wear in them. You are splashed getting in and getting out; and the wind takes your hair and your bonnet in every direction. I hate an open carriage myself' (Chap. 13, p.102).

Thus Catherine discovers Mr Allen's view, and Mrs Allen discovers her own thoughts on the subject. Catherine having been unaware that Mr Allen disapproved in any way. But here no comment from the author is needed to reinforce the irony; it exists in the non-communication and non-understanding of husband and wife, for just as, in *Pride and Prejudice*, Mr Bennet thinks of his wife's nerves as his constant companions over some twenty-five years, so here Mr Allen has learned that his wife's dress is more important than his words.

Sometimes in *Northanger Abbey* the irony and the satire are virtually indistinguishable. A good instance occurs early in the novel when, in her own voice, the author attacks the reviewers, following this with a brilliantly sustained elevation of the art of novel writing itself. Here she is being ironic about snobbery in literature:

And while the abilities of the nine-hundredth abridger of the *History of England*, or the man who collects and publishes in a volume some dozen lines of Milton, Pope, and Prior, with a paper from the *Spectator*, and a chapter from Sterne, are eulogized by a thousand pens, – there seems almost a general wish of decrying the capacity and undervaluing the labour of the novelist, and of slighting the performances which have only genius, wit, and taste to recommend them (Chapter 5, p.42).

This satirical-ironic tone colours all her writing about the Gothic novel, and is beautifully put into the mouth of Henry Tilney when he satirizes the manners of the fashionable young-man-about-Bath after the Master of Ceremonies has introduced him to Catherine. And Isabella refers to *Sir Charles Grandison* as 'an amazing horrid book', ironic in view of the fact that it endorses a strict code of morality by which she does not live. Irony through dialogue is always present when John Thorpe opens his uninformed mouth, for every boast is a comment on his lack of honesty and the inconsistent and arrogant mode of life he has adopted. Again there is a sly humour, even late in the novel, when the author regards the heroine she has set on the road to experience – imaginary and real – as a fortunate being who has by chance inherited the Gothicism she covets:

> With all the chances against her of house, hall, place, park, court and cottage, Northanger turned up an abbey, and she was to be its inhabitant. Its long, damp passages, its narrow cells and ruined chapel, were to be within her daily reach, and she could not entirely subdue the hope of some traditional legends, some awful memorials of an injured and ill-fated nun (Chap. 17, p.132).

The area of fantasy is ruthlessly exposed, as when Henry gently rebukes his sister for misunderstanding Catherine's fearful account of what is to happen, Eleanor thinking that she has been speaking of fact not fiction. While natural descriptions are undertaken with ease, the inner consciousness that is often thought to be the peculiar prerogative of the 20th-century novelist is very much Jane Austen's manner too. Catherine at the Abbey conducts many monologues with herself about the fearful things she thinks (half hopes) have happened, and sometimes the punctuation and the length of the sentences convey the nervous tension of the young girl destined to be a somewhat different kind of heroine. Dialogue, monologue or soliloquy are all of a piece in Jane Austen's writing, but what we have said earlier about her style, its precise and harmonious quality, must be here illustrated in an unsatirical mode. Note the flow, the balance, the ease of the writing.

> Returning through the large and lofty hall, they ascended a broad-staircase of shining oak, which, after many flights and many landing-places, brought them upon a long wide gallery. On one side it had a range of doors, and it was lighted on the other by windows which Catherine had only time to discover looked into a quadrangle, before Miss Tilney led the way into a chamber, and scarcely staying to hope she would find it comfortable, left her with an anxious entreaty that she would make as little alteration as possible in her dress (Chap. 20, p.151).

This is a particularly good example of Jane Austen's succinctness, because it conveys the sharp experience of arrival at a new place, the fleeting nature of that experience and, Eleanor's fear (almost unnoticed) that Catherine might be late and thus annoy her father. It brings us happily to a most important point about any reading of Jane Austen: the student cannot afford to read quickly (except on the first reading, when the narrative, the story, is most important) he must discipline himelf to weigh the significance of each word and phrase, and see it as a part of the jigsaw of the whole. Jane Austen's style encompasses with equal felicity the town settings of Bath and the country settings around Northanger:

> The remainder was shut off by knolls of old trees, or luxurious plantations, and the steep woody hills rising behind to give it shelter, were beautiful even in the leafless month of March (Chap. 22, p.164).

There is nothing symbolic about this, and Catherine's response is a natural one, free from associations and sensations that would belong to fiction rather than fact. Within Jane Austen's style, as we have seen, there is immense variety, and the antithetical balance and aphoristic turns that distinguish the work of Pope are sometimes to be found, as when she observes that 'Friendship is certainly the finest balm for the pangs of disappointed love.' It must be admitted, however, that such turns are not as common in *Northanger Abbey* as in some of the other novels, where the maturity of thought and expression combine in memorable aphorisms that exactly define her subject, as in the opening of *Pride and Prejudice*: 'It is a truth universally acknowledged, that a single man in possession of a good fortune, must be in want of a wife.'

Overt satire and irony, a fluent and natural command of dialogue and description, simplicity and directness of utterance are, in Jane Austen, reinforced in all the novels by a subtle power of suggestion or association that indicates to the reader the way things will ultimately turn out. In *Northanger Abbey* the General, while he has certain grotesque and humorous associations, is exposed to a subtle innuendo that indicates he is a mercenary and selfish man. Yet society might well accept him to be the reverse of this. Jane Austen's style leaves the reader, the discriminating reader, in no doubt, but the exact nature of the General's lack of honour is not revealed until the end.

The author's use of her own voice is a marked feature of her work. Her defence of the novel has been referred to earlier, but there are many other occasions, particularly at the beginning of the book, where she comments on her heroine, on society or on particular aspects of life. There is a certain intimacy thus established with the reader, but in *Northanger Abbey* it is never allowed to clog the narrative or to assume the proportions that it does, say, in Thackeray or Trollope or even in Dickens. In other words, the narrative flow – what will happen to Catherine, will her romance prosper or not – these are the main areas of interest and they are not allowed to flag. But in *Northanger Abbey* the main element of the style is a comic one for, as its author says, a novel contains 'the liveliest effusions of wit and humour', and these should be couched in 'the best chosen language'. In *Northanger Abbey* these definitions cohere to provide a work that is at once entertaining and instructive – instructive not in any pedantic weighting of that term, but instructive of life in its particulars and, however limited the range, in its generalities too.

Themes

The themes are sufficiently clear, and occupy three areas of interest. Firstly, there is the satire on the Gothic romance through the conversations the heroine has with Isabella, with Henry Tilney and his sister, and in passing with John Thorpe; also in the course of the inner dialogue she conducts with her own imagination, particularly at Northanger Abbey. Secondly, there is the appraisal of fashionable Bath society, not at an elevated level but at what today would be called a 'tourist' level, and this too is satirical in tone because of the essential superficiality involved. Thirdly, there is the moral theme, which has to do with the education of the heroine's feelings and mind, and which is closely linked to what we might call right conduct and an essentially moral way of life.

We must never forget that Jane Austen is a moral writer, and though it could be argued that Henry is not exactly a working clergyman, Jane Austen is very much concerned with what we ought to call the Christian code, which places a high premium on truthfulness and integrity and consideration for others. This code puts down pretentiousness and affectation, regards the retiring rather than the fashionable condition as being desirable, or at least commendable; suggests that humility is vastly superior to arrogance; disapproves of materialism and worldliness as distinct from the cultivation of the human spirit. The real moral stricture of General Tilney is that he worships false standards; the real moral worth of Catherine is that she speaks the truth both inwardly and outwardly and has the capacity to acknowledge self-error. The satirical-burlesque and the moral-Christian are thus the thematic constants of *Northanger Abbey*, and they provide the frame or structure within which the action operates.

General questions

1 Compare and contrast Isabella and John Thorpe, indicating clearly whether you consider there is a family likeness.

Guideline notes to be used in the answer:

(a) Introduction – Mrs Allen's meeting with and rediscovery of Mrs Thorpe – Catherine's dull life in Bath changed by meeting Isabella – subsequent arrival of John Thorpe and James Morland. Apparent good fortune of this – Isabella and James already known to each other – Catherine happy and secure in new relationship quickly.

(b) Isabella – character described (two paras) – talkative, ostentatious (quote), apparently warm and sincere, expressions of friendship (quote or reference), flirtatious and dishonest (the two young men, and later Captain Tilney), sophisticated in the ways of the world (compare Catherine's innocence), *selfish* (refer to at least two instances), cunning, loud, insincere, incapable of sticking to what she says, thoughtless of others (the journey/the Tilneys), obstinate, self-willed, arrogant, lacking core of morality etc. Quote or refer to text/instances wherever possible. Do not make unsupported statements.

(c) John – loud, brash (quote or refer), ignorant, likes the sound of his own voice, conceited, a constitutional liar (the time it takes to get from . . . compared with the reality), arrogant, insensitive (particularly to Catherine's needs), boastful (horses/carriages), egoistic (does what he wants), lacks a sense of humour, clumsy, ill-mannered, devious and inaccurate (conversation with General Tilney re Catherine), irresponsible, lack of moral core. (possibly two paragraphs, though they won't be as long as Isabella's).

(d) Conclusion – similarities – points to be taken from the above paras through instances in which Isabella and John act together (a) the drives or (b) separately *but* with similar attitudes – inconsiderate, irresponsible, silly, arrogant, loud etc.

2 Write an essay on the objects of Jane Austen's satire in *Northanger Abbey*, paying particular attention to the means she employs to achieve her effects.

3 Write a character study of Catherine Morland, referring closely to the text in support of your answer.

4 Write an account of life in Bath during this period, using only evidence drawn from this novel.

5 Write a detailed account of the types of humour employed by Jane Austen in this novel.

6 In what ways does Jane Austen defend the novel and how does *Northanger Abbey* itself illustrate that defence?

7 Examine in some detail one of the Gothic novels referred to in *Northanger Abbey*, and indicate whether you think Jane Austen's strictures are justified.

8 Write an appreciation of Jane Austen's use of dialogue in *Northanger Abbey*.

9 Compare and contrast the characters of Mrs Allen and Mrs Morland.

10 What, for you, are the most interesting aspects of Jane Austen's style in *Northanger Abbey*?

11 'She doesn't really like people.' How would you defend Jane Austen from this charge?

12 How does Jane Austen create a particular atmosphere in *Northanger Abbey*? You may refer to any two or three scenes in support of your answer.

13 In what ways is *Northanger Abbey* a 'moral novel'?

14 Write an appreciation of any two or three of the minor characters in the book, showing how Jane Austen brings them to life.

15 In what ways do you regard *Northanger Abbey* as a limited book? Give reasons for your answer.

16 In what ways is *Northanger Abbey* a 'wise' book?

17 Show how the feelings of Catherine Morland are educated during the course of the novel.

18 'It is merely a love-story.' Would you agree or disagree with this assessment of *Northanger Abbey*?

19 Examine the nature and variety of Jane Austen's irony in this novel.

20 'Slight.' Would you agree or disagree with this assessment of *Northanger Abbey* as a novel?

Further reading

Jane Austen: Facts and Problems, R. W. Chapman (OUP)

Selected Letters of Jane Austen, Ed. R. W. Chapman (OUP)

Jane Austen and Her Art, Mary Lascelles (OUP)

A Reading of Jane Austen: Barbara Hardy (Athlone Press 1979)

Other novels by Jane Austen (all Pan Books)
Sense and Sensibility
Pride and Prejudice
Persuasion
Mansfield Park
Emma

Brodie's Notes are also available for the above listed Austen titles